A PARISH AT WAR:
Letters from Nicaragua

A PARISH AT WAR:
LETTERS FROM NICARAGUA

by John Medcalf

Templegate Publishers
Springfield, Illinois

The greater part of this book was originally published by the Catholic Institute for International Relations, 22 Coleman Fields, London N1 7AF, England. Thanks are also due to The Tablet (London) and The Catholic Herald (London) for use of material which originally appeared in their pages.

Manufactured in the United States of America

Templegate Publishers, 302 E. Adams St., Springfield, IL 62701

ISBN 0-87243-182-7

The designs on the cover and throughout the text are taken from fragments of pre-Columbian Central American pottery.

Foreword

by Graham Greene

Since 1980 I have been visiting Nicaragua nearly every year, but I have learnt all I know of the dangerous contra central area on the way to the Atlantic coast from Father Medcalf's letters. These describe daily life in a small parish with the rather odd name of Muelle de los Bueyes (Ox-ford) where contra attacks which spare neither women or children are just a part of normal life.

> Hardly a day passes without an ambush, a skirmish or exploding mines. On July 3 a Franciscan brother, Tomás Zavaleta (40) was killed when his jeep was blown up by an anti-tank mine, and the parish priest Father Ignacio (30) was gravely injured. Twelve of our parishioners from Jacinto Baca were mown down by contra machine-gunners a week ago.
>
> 18th of November 1987. Two houses away from this parish church the three young daughters of the man who sells rum and cigarettes were all wounded in the legs by shrapnel; one of them may never walk again. In comparison the five-inch wide hole in my tin roof was nothing.

I take these two quotations at random. Under these conditions Father Medcalf, in order to take advantage of the literacy campaign in 1979, started a travelling library — not of books devoted to Marxist economics as President Reagan would claim. Nicaragua is a country of poets.

Last year I asked Father Cardenal, the Minister of Education, to help me visit Father Medcalf and he bluntly refused. 'The route is far too dangerous,' he told me, 'and we would feel responsible.' They had taken me some years before to the Honduras border, but Ox-ford no! Impossible!

How glad I am that at least for a while Father Medcalf is out of danger.

EDITOR'S NOTE

John Medcalf is a Roman Catholic priest born in Canterbury, England who spent 15 years in parishes in Peru before going to Nicaragua for three years. His parishioners in the villages of Ox-ford, Monkey Face, Washtub and The Laurels are described in these circular letters which he wrote as part of his attempt "to make known the justice of their case". They were written from late 1985 to late 1989 and describe many aspects of the place and the people of rural Nicaragua during a time when the US government was voting through millions in aid to the contras. The letters were published in newspapers in Britain, France, Spain, Germany and Ireland.

There are descriptions of the country with its flora and fauna; 11 species of butterflies that he saw in an hour; the variety of orchids; the quetzal he didn't see, an exotic long-tailed bird said to be one of the most beautiful in the world; the king vulture and the keel-billed toucan; the macaws and howler monkeys; the danto or tapir; the sloth and the ever present cicadas. This place with black soil where coffee, maize, onions and tomatoes are grown, and bananas, breadfruit, coconuts, oranges, lemons, grapefruit and passion fruit. Where people eat rice and beans, and boiled beef and tortillas on special days, and share chicken and rum on a fiesta. Where they make multicoloured wreaths of paper flowers, play street games, watch a circus family of five and a monkey, hold festivals for Christmas and Easter, and listen to the World Cup. Where half the population of 3 million is under 15, and most of the young men are in the army.

He is amazed by the Nicaraguan spirit; that the people do not fall prey to despair; that their troubles have not extinguished acts of kindness but have probably increased them. That here God comes first and that He is the God of the poor. That "nobody is surrendering over here" (Aquí No Se Rinde Nadie). Whether in Managua, Bluefields or in the rural comarcas or regions, the principles of justice are within the grasp of an entire nation. "You have won your freedom, small land of greatness" said one of their poets.

John Medcalf's job was to set up Rural Libraries as part of a literacy campaign, to help those who had recently learned to read to keep up their skill. There were usually about 20 books and two tables in a palm thatched hut, but they were important and welcomed in each village. He officiated at marriages and baptisms, found confessions in wartime most difficult, often said Mass for hundreds of his parishioners to the accompaniment of folk music, played the violin badly and walked more than 200 miles in fifteen days on a Way of the Cross for Peace and Life to publicise the peasant church to the outside world. Seven men did the entire route in their wheelchairs, just a few of the thousands of war-wounded in Nicaragua. He rode horseback around the villages with his native guide, met the contras on several occasions, and received threats warning him "not to be manipulated by the atheistic hordes," as the contras called the campesinos or peasant farmers in his parishes. He slept in a hammock, marveled at the beauty of the jungle and the jasmine after a tropical storm, went to the Book Fair in Managua, discussed the spirituality of Liberation Theology and tended the blood-soaked injured and dead in his parish hall after a contra raid.

He saw the village co-operatives of Rio Rama and Fernando Salazar charred and gutted. In his first letter he describes the ever present danger in which the villagers live. He arrived to say his first Mass in Caro de Mono, "but the contras had got there first". Nearly one hundred heavily armed mercenaries had come out of the rain-forest to capture the village. One soldier, seventeen years old, had had his head blown off by a grenade; a midwife had repelled the attack single-handedly with a sub-machine gun. The war was like a huge garishly painted backcloth of blood and sacrifice with the massive involvement of the United States so apparent. But there was a counter-balancing idealism and effort of the young, as visitors and helpers, and as campaigners abroad in the United States and Europe and worldwide.

He thought of the parallel of the Hebrews enslaved in Egypt; of David and Goliath; of the story of Jonah and the Whale, Jonah called by God to warn the people of Nineveh City to repent. He meditated on the Beatitudes as he met more and more people who, he is convinced, are simply, but certainly, Blessed.

He met catechists, farmers, nuns, families, elders, children, shopkeepers, coffee pickers, volunteers, prelates, politicians, musicians, soldiers and civilians throughout El Salvador, Guatemala and Nicaragua.

July 1, 1989 marked the tenth anniversary of the Nicaraguan Revolution. The violence of the contras and the October hurricane of 1988 have left Bluefields and the Atlantic coastline devastated.

The reader of these letters will be moved to question seriously the notorious "backyard policy" of successive US administrations in their dealings with Central America. The indictment by the Catholic bishops of the United States in 1987 that US policies are "seriously flawed" is amply borne out by the battlefield letters of Father John Medcalf.

Preface

I wish to acknowledge gratefully the work of those who distributed these letters or facilitated their publication in newspapers, magazines or on radio programs. They are too many to remember, but chief among them are Robert Copsey, Kathy Doust (my sister), Mike Simpson and the Archdeacons of Winchester (a family, not a clutch of clergy).

I dedicate the book especially to those who continue the struggle for survival and peace in Central Zelaya. Jorge Vélez and Paddy Welsh are remembered in the text of the letters, as is Padre Bernard Boulang, my successor as parish priest of Oxford, whose efforts for reconciliation are exceptional. The three parish sisters from Green Bay (irreverently dubbed by me 'Pink Creek'), Mary, Helen, Agnes, are rightly known for their perseverance and their personal valour, and I love them all equally in different ways.

Finally, but chiefly, I dedicate these letters to the thirty thousand or so peasant farmers of the parish of Muelle de los Bueyes, whose suffering and love are known to God alone. May they soon know real peace.

All proceeds from this book will go to CIIR development projects in Nicaragua.

John Medcalf

August 1988

1985

Muelle de los Bueyes
("Ox-ford")
Nicaragua
27 November 1985

Dear Friends,

I write this letter in the fond hope that it may arrive before the situation here becomes desperate.

After less than a month in Nicaragua, I find myself in Cristo Redentor parish, in a small town called Muelle de los Bueyes (which means Ox-ford, but there are no university spires) on the chief link road between the Pacific and Atlantic oceans.

In the last week this area has become the main focus of combat between the local Sandinista army and the US-backed contras. This parish house may well be turned into a casualty hospital within a day or so.

Last Sunday I was scheduled to say mass at 2 pm in the village of Cara de Mono, but the contras got there first. At 12:30 about 100 heavily-armed mercenaries burst out of the tropical rain-forest and tried to capture the village. There was heavy cross-fire immediately behind the Catholic chapel, and the first to die was Iván Torres, a 17-year old villager fighting with the Sandinistas. From the parish house here in Muelle, only 10 kilometers from Cara de Mono, we clearly heard the machine-gun fire. Fr. José Curcio (the parish priest) and myself reached the village at 3:30 and discovered that the mercenaries had been driven off; 19 of them had been killed and many others severely wounded. The Sandinista Air Force had sent in three small reconnaissance planes and two troop carrier helicopters, and the village resembled an outsized wasp nest. My most poignant memory of that Sunday afternoon was the horrified grief of the young brothers of Iván Torres, whose head had been blown off by a grenade.

The village catechist is a woman who also belongs to the Sandinista police. She described how her house had been surrounded by a group of contras, and how she had repelled the attack single-handedly, with a sub-machine gun. Her prompt action must have saved the village from a blood-bath. The high morale and great bravery of Nicaraguans like Amanda is what distinguishes the Sandinista cause.

Since the contra attack on Sunday afternoon there have been reports of build-up of forces on both sides. One of the six parish deacons came in yesterday to the parish house; 80 mercenaries had passed within a few yards of his small holding. His fear was all the more understandable when I learned that his teenage daughter was taken as a hostage to Costa Rica a few months ago, where she was repeatedly raped before eventually escaping. Another of our deacons is on a contra blacklist, because of his adherence to the Sandinista militia; his house has been burned once, and there have been two attempts on his life.

Not everybody here supports the Sandinista government, of course. Most of the shopkeepers and commercial travellers have seen their living standards eroded and would welcome a change at the top. It is not difficult, however, to discern that a large majority of the population supports the present leadership. In the most carefully monitored of Latin American elections the Sandinistas polled just over two-thirds of the vote in November last year. Even the third who did not support them would not all be in favour of a violent overthrow of the elected government. There is a parliamentary opposition which is consulted on a wide range of affairs.

In many ways we are living from one day to the next, without a clear vision of the way things will work out. The massive involvement of the US in trying to destroy what its leaders regard as communism is yet another major error on the part of the Reagan administration. The silence and compliance of most of the Nicaraguan bishops is perhaps no worse than the performance of the German bishops when faced with Nazism 50 years ago, but it is equally unpalatable. Who is to condemn our deacons and catechists for taking up arms to defend their families and their freedoms? Does 61-year old Father Curcio act wrongly by publicly declaring his readiness to fight alongside the youths of his parish against the American invaders? I don't think so. And I am sure that in war-torn Nicaragua, and in all of Central America, God has taken sides, just as he took the side of the enslaved Hebrews in Ancient Egypt. God is visible in the faces of the poor who are struggling for a better life, a life without fear and hunger.

Please give these people the support they deserve, by making known the justice of their cause.

God bless you,

Padre Juan Luis
(John Medcalf)

("Ox-ford")
Muelle de los Bueyes
Nicaragua
14 December 1985

Dear Friends,

Sunday 1 December: Said mass in two villages (Presilla and Diamante); 35 killings in Presilla and five in Diamante in the last three weeks . . . repeated attempts by contra mercenaries to take these villages, all unsuccessful so far; post-office burned and gutted, as well as three vehicles belonging to State organisations . . . villagers robbed of watches, money, clothes; hostages taken but later released.

Monday 2 December: Fourteen young Sandinista soldiers killed north of here when their helicopter shot down by 'Sam 7' missiles (supplied to contras by USA): serious escalation of war.

Wednesday 4 December: 30,000 Nicaraguans protested 'Sam 7' killings in Managua's 19 de Julio Plaza this morning (the BBC Overseas Service reported that 'about one hundred persons protested' and failed to mention the US involvement!)

Saturday 7 December: Today is the Eve of the Immaculate Conception of Mary, and traditionally the most important fiesta in the year throughout Nicaragua. Choirs of children roam the streets of the villages singing religious songs in front of flower-bedecked altars, receiving sweets and fruit for their labours. Tonight it is difficult to remember this country is at war. The Sandinista Government has gone to great pains to promote this fiesta, even to the extent of giving prizes for the most artistic altars. Fireworks explode all through the night, and newcomers like myself might be forgiven for confusing them with rifle shots or machine-gun fire.

Tuesday 10 December: We learned today that all bridges along our only road have been mined by the Sandinista army. It seems that this is the only effective way to prevent our region falling completely into the hands of the mercenaries. Unfortunately, there have been two victims in Presilla village: a 12-year old boy was killed when he climbed the barbed-wire to retrieve a 100-cordoba note (worth 13 US cents) and a young Sandinista recruit who tried to hold him back. (Two days later: the 100-cordoba note is still there.)

Thursday 12 December: At approx. 9:30 this morning, a mine exploded at the bridge nearest our village of Muelle de los Bueyes, shaking all our houses. Two people were killed — a young woman and an 18-year old deaf and dumb Sandinista soldier. I knew the soldier; his name was Concepción (he must have been born on December 8) or Conchito for short, and he came to my evening mass just two days ago . . . his face was an uninterrupted smile as we communicated with signs, his pistol hung from his belt and I remember wondering whether he was the only deaf-and-dumb soldier in the Sandinista army. He received Holy Communion with a devotion that made me feel ashamed of my own luke-warmness. And now he's dead . . . yet another victim of Reagan's bullying. At 5 pm the Secretario Político addressed a public meeting in the church hall; he explained the reasons for mining the bridges and warned the people — and especially the children — to keep away from the barbed wire. (The fears are greatest in areas like La Batea, where the bridges are very close to the centres of population. It seems that a pig and a dog have already been killed by mines in La Batea.)

Friday 13 December: More deaths a few miles to the east, where the contras staged one of their few successful ambushes; between four and eight soldiers killed. Tonight we had an open-air concert of music, theatre and folk-dancing from a travelling troupe of Nicaraguans accompanied by two Dutch 'internationalists'. Somehow life and love flourish in the middle of death and war. Central American Peace March began in Panama yesterday, led by Willy Brandt & Jesse Jackson, with messages from Graham Greene, etc. . . we need more of this sort of thing to keep world opinion fixed on the crimes being committed daily against these lovely people.

God bless

Padre Juan Luis Medcalf

1986

'Cristo Redentor'
Muelle de los Bueyes
(''Ox-ford'')
Nicaragua

9 February 1986

Dear Friends,

Much has happened since my two 'war dispatches' of November and December. Most of it is good news.

Shortly before Christmas the contras withdrew from this area, giving us the best possible Christmas present: PEACE. Now, six weeks later, the bridges are still mined and the villages still heavily guarded, but there have been no major combats. Victory? Tactical withdrawal? It's anybody's guess.

Meanwhile, I have decided to press ahead with the Rural Libraries Project which I began in Peru 15 years ago, and which is the chief reason for my being now in Nicaragua. The decision was taken three weeks ago. I had gone to say the monthly mass at Cara de Mono, where 17-year old Iván Torres had been killed when the contras attacked his village on November 24.

The small chapel was crowded. There were armed soldiers from the ragged Sandinista army, lots of children sitting on the cool tiled floor, and the few benches were occupied by the village elders. And Iván's mother was there. It was one of the most joyful religious celebrations I have ever known. Two guitarists accompanied the singing of the moving Misa Campesina, by Carlos Mejía Godoy, Nicaragua's foremost musician. The text of this Ordinary of the mass gives a dazzling portrayal of the flora and fauna of this country of volcanoes, lakes and tropical rainforest, with the Risen Christ right in the centre, living in the hearts and faces of the three and a half million human beings who struggle here for survival. There is nothing comparable that I know of in the English language.*

The 'sermon' was a conversation, a dialogue about the need for Hope. I had chosen this theme, because I expected to find the villagers of Cara de Mono downcast, perhaps despondent, after all they had gone through in 1985. I don't yet know the

**The text is given on pages 101-108.*

Nicaraguan spirit! The dialogue was buoyant, with occasional flashes of real humour. The mother of Iván said that her son's death had given a new spirit to the village. Others agreed.

— They thought we had yellow livers, but we had them running like centipedes!
— The other villagers won't laugh at us in the future. ('Cara de Mono' means 'Monkey-Face', so they have reason to laugh!)
— Iván Torres was like Jesus Christ; he died, but he's living here present amongst us today. It's not how *long* you live that matters, it's *how* you live and *how* you die.

And so on. I mentioned my interest in Rural Libraries, adding that men and women who had learned to read should not become illiterate through disuse of the skill. The idea was pounced upon. They wanted a library almost at once (with a chess-board, dominoes and newspapers, as well as books). It would be named after Iván Torres and would have his framed photograph in a place of honor.

Since that day two other villages have also requested a Rural Library. A small 'committee for cultural activities' has been formed in each village, and they inform me of their progress in looking for a piece of land or a house for sale. Because of the war, property is cheap.

What really amazes me is the spirit of optimism in these people, in spite of a war of aggression that is far from finished. Hope was born for them on 19 July 1979, when for the first time in their history the Christian principles of justice in which they believe were suddenly within the grasp of the entire nation.

I enclose a few photographs. I am grateful for the many letters from different parts and I pass on your thoughts, wishes and assurance of prayers to the peasant-farmers of Nicaragua.

God be with you all

Padre Juan Luis Medcalf

Parroquia Cristo Redentor
Muelle de los Bueyes
("Ox-ford")
Nicaragua
4 March 1986

Dear Friends,

I have just walked 205 miles and am nursing my feet!

The initiative came from Father Miguel D'Escoto, the Nicaraguan Foreign Minister. Just before the beginning of Lent he issued an invitation to Christians all over the country to join him in a Way of the Cross for Peace and Life. This Lenten practice is normally restricted to the Catholic tradition, but many Baptists, Methodists and Anglicans were among the pilgrims.

The peregrination lasted 15 days. The starting-point (or First Station) was the long-suffering border town of Jalapa, a mere four miles from Honduran territory. Although only 120 persons promised to make the entire journey by foot, we were joined en route by hundreds and then thousands of men, women and children willing to walk for a shorter period. Most of the marchers were peasants who have suffered the loss of relatives or property in the five-year war. One 72-year old farmer had witnessed the deaths of eight grandchildren at the hands of the contras. Seven men did the entire Way of the Cross in their wheelchairs. They were just a few of the thousands of war-wounded in Nicaragua.

The border towns were understandably more active in their support of the religious march. We were often given the welcome accorded to a liberation army: Beans and rice, cool drinks and a place to sleep at night were never lacking during the first half of the journey. The Bishop of Estelí opened his cathedral and celebrated a liturgy with Padre Miguel D'Escoto, giving his blessing to crowds who had come to doubt whether any of the nine Nicaraguan bishops would ever risk the wrath of the Cardinal Primate of Managua by supporting this Way of the Cross.

Towards the end of the route, two priests had shut the doors of their churches to the pilgrims. Peasant sacristans countermanded their clergy by opening the church doors at the arrival of the singing crowds, thereby almost certainly losing their jobs and their sustenance.

The culmination of two weeks of dusty roads and sun-parched tracks was the final mass in Managua's Plaza de la Revolución on Friday 28 February. Concelebrated by 73 priests (there are only 310 in the entire country, including the infirm and the retired). And attended by at least 20,000 faithful, this religious gathering was possibly the biggest show of strength to date of the 'church of the poor' as it is being dubbed. Father Miguel D'Escoto is not permitted by the Holy See to say mass, because of his political office, but he was the principal speaker in a 3-hour ceremony that was broadcast and televised live from the Plaza. He reminded us that the chief objective of this unusual Way of the Cross had been to storm heaven (and Washington?) for an end to the war that has taken 11,000 lives in five years. We stood in silence remembering the four Nicaraguan mothers and the Swiss volunteer bricklayer, 29-year old Maurice Damierre, who had all been killed by contra bullets on the third day of the march. Fr. D'Escoto said:

> "We are nothing less than the Roman, Catholic and Apostolic church of Nicaragua. We are not a parallel church, as is asserted by those who are afraid to denounce the systematic murder of our people. We are a church that loves and needs its bishops, and calls out to them to stand by their people in this hour of aggression. We appeal, we implore that they decide once and for all whether they support the God of death and war, or the God of life and peace."

Was the Cardinal watching us on his television? Will the multitudinous ceremony have moved him closer to the anguish of Nicaragua's refugees and peasants, or will he react by strengthening an even closer alliance with the middle and upper classes whom he defends and who lost their power in 1979?

During the Way of the Cross we were joined by numerous foreign delegations—a Swedish Lutheran Bishop, a handful of British church leaders headed by the Dean of St. Paul's Cathedral London; a group of Brazilian Catholics prominent in their country's Basic Christian Communities; and priests and pastors from Alaska and Vermont. Messages of solidarity arrived from Cardinal Lorscheider of Brazil, Bishop Méndez Arceo of Mexico, and others.

We are conscious that what is happening in the largest of the Central American republics is having repercussions well beyond its frontiers. Fr. D'Escoto has publicly condemned the Soviet occupation of Afghanistan, hardly the best evidence that Nicaragua is a Marxist satellite of Moscow. The only real religious persecution is that unleashed by the Cardinal himself, who has expelled, by 'termination of contract', over 60 priests and numerous religious sisters for their defence of the Sandinista Revolution.

In this part of the world, at least, as Holy Week and Easter come nearer, there is a growing sense of the re-enactment of Christ's own passion, death and resurrection. Is the Christian message just an individual recipe for salvation and personal happiness, or does it imply also the changing of unjust political structures so that there is no more starvation in Ethiopia, no more bullying in Poland, no more genocide in El Salvador and Nicaragua?

The answers to these religious questions are a matter of life and death.

May God bless, guide and enlighten us all.

Padre Juan Luis Medcalf

Parroquia Cristo Redentor
Muelle de los Bueyes
("Ox-ford")
Nicaragua

10 April 1986

Dear Friends,

March is 'back-to-school' month in Nicaragua. We have 62 schools in our rural parish, but this year only 40 are functioning. The others—in remote villages, populated by maize-growing farmers—are closed because the contras have murdered the teachers.

I have spent a good part of the month visiting the schools that remain open. The children are remarkably resilient, even those who have witnessed rape, torture and assassination. They and their teachers expect me to lead prayers for the dead, to say mass for an end to hostilities, and to give encouragement and hope. The pastoral freedom I experience as a priest in Nicaragua belies the outrageous accusation made by the Reagan administration that there is 'religious persecution' in this country.

The month of March was also characterised by the campaign in Washington for a hundred million dollars, to finance the war against the Sandinista government. As I visited the isolated one-teacher schools set in a landscape of palm-trees and volcanic hills, I was haunted by the faces of the children. If Reagan gets his money, many of them will not reach adulthood or even adolescence.

One parent put it to me succinctly and truthfully when he said: 'The super-powers experiment with *their* bombs and with *our* blood.'

This extraordinary preoccupation with education in the middle of a vicious war of aggression is another testimony to the special qualities of the Sandinistas. Illiteracy is treated like any other disease: to be eliminated as quickly and as painlessly as possible, so that the nation can stand on its own feet and short-cut the path to progress for all.

We inaugurated our first rural library on Sunday April 6, in Cara de Mono ("Monkey Face"). Some of you will remember that this village was attacked on November 24 last year, days after my arrival in the parish. The library is named after Iván Torres, the 17-year old killed in the battle. His mother, Maria, gave a little speech before cutting the pink ribbon across the doorway:

> "My son is living still. I know it. He is living with us, especially in this small library that has grown out of his dead body. If I could give birth to more sons like Iván, to die for our revolution, I would gladly, gladly do it . . ."

The villagers cheered and clapped—and wept. Iván's photograph hangs over the chess table in the new building that cost less than £250 to buy and about the same sum again to fit out with a few basic books (agriculture, first aid, children's stories, a dictionary, a bible, etc.). Representatives from eight other villages were at the inaugural ceremony; all of them are now clamouring for their own Village Library. If we can raise the money we shall find ourselves with plenty of inaugurations in the months ahead.

Incidentally, we built a small concrete stage outside the library, which means that we have an outdoor theatre as well. Amateur dramatic societies, roving musicians and other popular entertainers will have a venue and an enthusiastic public in Cara de Mono from now on.

I had very little time for sleep in Holy Week. In Nicaragua shops, offices and schools close for the entire week (religious persecution?!), and not just for two days. The people spilled onto the streets for multitudinous processions on Palm Sunday complete with real donkeys and real palms. Men and women alternated to carry an exaggeratedly heavy wooden cross through the villages on Good Friday. On Holy Saturday traditional bonfires blazed for hours outside the churches in the darkness that precedes the dawn of Easter. Sermons, I felt, were superfluous: these people know more about death and hope and living Christianity than their shepherd who walks with them.

I had hoped to finish this letter in a major key, of optimism. However, a nun of this diocese, Sandra Price from California, gave me a written report yesterday. The following excerpts need no comment from me:

> "On March 25 a group of contras took one of our Catholic catechists, Donato Mendoza, from his home, two kilometres further on they castrated him, gouged out his eyes, pulled out his fingernails, cut the flesh from his legs, broke every bone in his body, and shot him . . .

Three days later, on Good Friday, his naked, mutilated body was found. Donato had always worn a chain and cross, as a distinctive mark of his position in the church. He said he had lost the cross a few days before while working. It was this chain without a cross that identified his dead body. He no longer wore a cross of metal; his life had taken on the passion and death of Jesus.

On Easter Sunday we celebrated mass with Donato's family: mother, brothers, sister, wife, nine children, two grandchildren. On the altar was the chain, matted with blood and dirt. There was no cross. As Christ's life did not terminate on the cross but in the victory of the resurrection, so, too, we believe that Donato has conquered death and suffering, and lives on by the power of this same God whom he served faithfully during the 40 years of his life."

Sincerely,

Padre Juan Luis (Medcalf)

Parroquia Cristo Redentor
Muelle de los Bueyes
("Ox-ford")
Nicaragua

11 May 1986

Dear Friends,

In Central America May is the month of butterflies. They suddenly appeared one day last week, in an astonishing range of sizes and patterns, like so many coloured telegrams announcing peace for Nicaragua. I watched the children in Cara de Mono village running excitedly after them, without any apparent intention of capturing or harming the exotic insects. The new sport came to an abrupt finish when a tropical storm sent children and butterflies in search of dry shelter.

It is just one year since the US government cut off all trading links with Nicaragua. The effects of this embargo are seen in the near-empty supermarkets of Managua, and in the creative improvisation that keeps battered Fords and rusting Massey-Fergusons still functioning in spite of the unavailability of spare parts. Here in the rural areas we are less affected by the shortages, since many basic food-stuffs are grown locally. The Sandinista government has introduced rationing for a wide range of goods, and imposes heavy penalties on those who hoard or speculate. Consequently there is fairness in the distribution and most people seem to accept the shortages rather as the British did during World War II. It is interesting to note that one of the more dynamic members of the Sandinista cabinet, Jaime Wheelock (Minister of Agriculture, and therefore responsible for food supply and distribution), is the grandson of an English coffee planter.

On 26 April, nine soldiers were killed in a contra ambush just a few miles from Muelle de los Bueyes. Four of these were local lads and their bodies were brought to the parish church for an all-night 'wake'. The simple coffins lay before the altar as I said the Requiem mass. Anger and sadness competed inside me as I witnessed once again the faces of mothers tortured with sorrow.

A few readers of my letters have accused me of being 'one-sided'. I make no claim to political objectivity. I report what I witness and what I experience, and try to avoid a selective presentation of the evidence.

An Irish reader remarked that 'the Nicaraguan war will be lost or won not in Nicaragua but in the streets of Europe, where resistance to Washington's policies must be maintained vigorously'. I agree.

I began this letter with butterflies; I wish to end it with a flower. What is happening in this small republic is a delicate orchid unclassified by botanists. It is attacked from right and left. Only a few weeks ago Eli Altamirano, president of the Nicaraguan Communist Party, declared '...the Sandinistas are ideologically promiscuous. They have priests, nuns, evangelicals and bourgeois in their government. It has nothing to do with Marxism-Leninism.'

The following is my attempt to translate one of C. Mejía Godoy's best-loved songs. It expresses, in poetry, what I have tried to convey in prose:

> Dear Nicaragua, small land of greatness, young, fragile orchid of rich perfume, your black earth drenched by blood of martyrs in search of freedom, fighting for peace and home. Dear Nicaragua, your lakes and forests mean more to me than foreign gold, but the fact that you've won your freedom, small land of greatness, means I love you so much more.

Sincerely,

Padre Juan Luis
(John Medcalf)

Parroquia Cristo Redentor
Muelle de los Bueyes
("Ox-ford")
Nicaragua
12 June 1986

Dear Friends,

Thanks to the help given or promised by readers of these letters, our team of three internationalists is now working in five villages, organising or building Rural Libraries. Jorge Vélez is a Peruvian teacher of drama; Patrick Welsh is a computer engineer from Scotland who worked for two years in Nigeria as a member of the Volunteer Missionary Movement; I split my time between the Library program and parish duties.

The five villages are large by Nicaraguan standards, with about 200 families in each, and have all (excepting Muelle) been the victims of contra attacks in the last year.

1 **Cara de Mono ("Monkey Face")** This is the only library fully functioning. Small children play ludo and read story-books. Sandinista militia play guitars and chess when off duty. Last week I saw two uniformed soldiers playing with wooden spinning-tops; each soldier was no more than 14 years old. Their childhood is yet another casualty of this six-year old aggression financed by US taxpayers. In this village even Amanda, the middle-aged midwife, slings a machine-gun over her shoulder when visiting her patients.

2 **Los Laureles** In spite of its pastoral name, 'The Laurels' has known little peace. It was just outside this village that eight Germans were kidnapped on May 17 this year. They are all young volunteers who came to this country to assist in a housing construction program for farmworkers. Fortunately they were handed back unharmed a few days ago. The people of The Laurels are passionately interested in their own folk-music, and the Rural Library, already partly finished, will cater in a special way to the 30 or so persons who play instruments or write songs. (Unfortunately all of them are men.)

3 **La Batea** Nobody seems to know why this village is called 'The Washtub', all the more strange since it

suffers from a chronic shortage of water. This is a very divided community, largely because of a number of wealthy farmers who disapprove of the government's 'interference' in matters of food production. They are all fervent Catholics who sing hymns loudly and out-of-tune (Do music and politics relate?). It is the poor majority who want a Rural Library, but it is proving difficult to unite the villagers sufficiently to begin building. A year ago, five soldiers were killed defending The Washtub.

4 **El Coral** This is not a necklace, but a venomous snake found in the area. On May 12 the contras made a cowardly attack on two families living just outside the village. Six were killed outright and eight (including three children) gravely wounded. A woman was shot for refusing to betray her husband's whereabouts. Their crime: unwillingness to spy on their neighbours. The people of El Coral are forming a Committee of Culture to discuss how they envisage their Rural Library, and where to build it (El Coral is a long, winding street resembling a snake).

5 **Muelle de los Bueyes** In Ox-ford the greatest hope lies in the Women's Sewing Cooperative. In a village of shopkeepers disgruntled with the official down-grading of shopkeeping, commercial advertising and consumerism, the women are beacons of light and progress. By organising themselves into a cooperative they have not only increased their family income, but have also arranged educational programs which will have long-reaching results. We are giving this group a lot of our time. Vilma, their leading lady, is a pillar of her evangelical church as well as a convinced Sandinista.

In the rest of Nicaragua the killings continue unabated. Victims of a landmine on May 27 were nine farmworkers and a Spanish volunteer doctor, Ambrosio Mogarrón, an expert on leprosy. His scientific and humanitarian work will be missed greatly.

A nation-wide debate is taking place publicly over the new Nicaraguan Constitution. It is impressive to see how different sectors of the population (teachers, civil servants, manual workers, Christians, etc.) attend their local town halls and suggest amendments or demand changes. This is no totalitarian state.

Meanwhile, the World Cup in Mexico assures Latin America of a momentary escape from reality as well as a little publicity on other continents.

God bless you,

Affectionately,
Padre Juan Luis Medcalf

Parroquia
Muelle de los Bueyes
("Ox-ford")
Nicaragua

20 June 1986

Dear Friends,

My attendance earlier this month at the 7th Annual Study Week of the Diocese of Bluefields prompted me to present this 'Portrait of a Nicaraguan Diocese in 1986'(see the table on pp. 30-31).

Appropriately enough, the theme of the lectures and discussions was 'Latin American Church History'. We examined the attitudes of Christians in two periods crucial for this country: the conquest by Spain after 1492, and the wars of independence at the beginning of the last century. Division within the church was every bit as acrimonious then as it is in the present crisis. In both previous conflicts the pope and most of the bishops made political judgments (against the interests of the indigenous population and in favour of the King of Spain) which are now condemned as un-Christian.

I was greatly and pleasantly surprised to discover that a large majority of my colleagues (26 out of 33) supports the Sandinista revolution that the US administration wishes to destroy. The support is greater among non-US citizens and is more pronounced among nuns and deacons than among priests. Supporters tend to be younger, more widely-travelled, and better educated. They are more likely to be working in the poorest sectors of the diocese.

The diocese of Bluefields includes half the national territory (the eastern half), but contains only one-tenth of the Nicaraguan population. Spanish Capuchin missionaries were replaced in the 1940s by American Capuchins from Wisconsin. The two bishops (one is a suffragan or auxiliary) are also American citizens.

Readers will perhaps resent the bluntness of the option 'for or against the Sandinista revolution'. I can offer no brief explanation. This country is at war, and in wartime citizens (Christian citizens as well) take sides. Although there was no mud-slinging at the Study Week, this was due more, I felt, to the uneven strength of the two sides than to any lack of passion. There was the constant feeling that 'X is one of us' and 'Y cannot be trusted'. Each of the 13 parishes had recited a litany of contra torture, sequestration and death that would have caused the Spanish conquistadors to blush.

It all reminded me of a description given me once by a Belgian priest of his seminary under the German occupation of World War II. The student priests were completely polarized on the question of the occupation: The Flemish-speakers were pro-Nazi and saw the Germans as their Teutonic cousins, whereas the French-speaking Walloons joined the resistance and were anti-German to a man. Neutrality was as impossible for them as it is for us.

Naturally there are degrees of support and of opposition. Parishes that are divided (like my own) have to tread more cautiously. I present the statistics without having had the benefit of a sociologist's advice. My hope is that they may help to clarify what is happening here, and elicit interest, action and prayer for a war-weary nation.

Affectionately,

Padre Juan Luis Medcalf

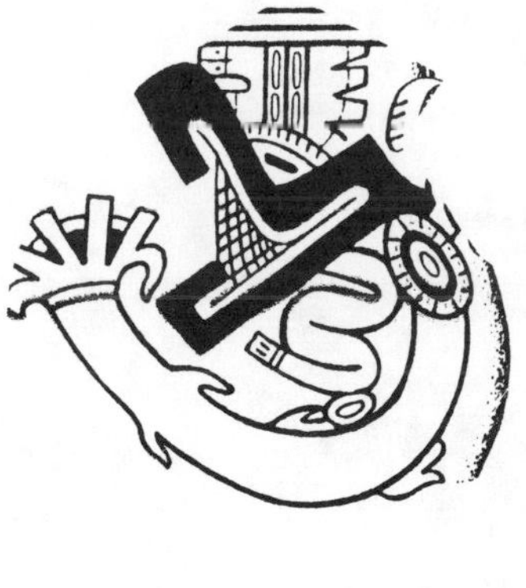

PORTRAIT OF A NICARAGUAN DIOCESE IN 1986

Parish	Full-time Personnel	Attitude To The Sandinista Revolution For + or Against —	(P)resent or (A)bsent in Study Week 1986
1 Bluefields	1 Bishop (USA)	—	PRESENT FOR 1 DAY
	5 Priests (3 USA	— — —	P A A
	1 Nicaragua	+	P
	1 Mexico)	—	A
	5 Sisters (2 Mexico	+ +	
	1 USA	+	
	1 Colombia	+	P P P A A
	1 Nicaragua)	+	
	1 Deacon (Nicaragua)	+	A
2 Puerto Cabezas	1 Bishop (USA)	—	A
	2 Priests (USA)	— —	A A
	3 Sisters (1 USA	+	A
	2 Nicaragua)	+ —	A A
3 Bonanza	1 Priest (USA)	—	P
	2 Sisters (Nicaragua)	?? (UNVERIFIED)	A A
4 Cukra Hill	3 Sisters (Nicaragua)	+ + +	P P A
5 LaCruz de Rio Grande	1 Priest (USA)	+	P
6 La Palma Africana	3 Priests (2 USA		
	1 Nicaragua)	+ + +	P A A
7 Muelle de los Bueyes	2 Priests (Canada, UK)	+ +	A P
	2 Sisters (USA)	— +	P P
8 Nueva Guinea	1 Priest (USA)	—	P
	2 Sisters (Brazil)	+ +	P P
9 Paiwas	1 Priest (USA)	+	P
	2 Sisters (Santo Domingo)	+ +	P P
10 Rama	3 Priests (USA)	— — —	A A P
	4 Sisters (Nicaragua)	+ — — —	P P A A
	1 Deacon	+	P
11 Rositas	2 Priests (Mexico	+	
	Nicaragua)	+	P P
	2 Sisters (USA	+	
	Nicaragua)	+	A A
12 Siuna	2 Priests (Nicaragua)	+ +	P P
	4 Sisters (1 USA	+	
	3 Nicaragua)	+ + +	P P P A
13 Waslala	1 Priest (Nicaragua)	+	P
	2 Sisters (Brazil)	+ +	P P
	Totals	+39	P33
		—18	A28

Summary of Attitudes

For the Sandinista Revolution +

Against —

Countries of Origin				Positions held			
Nicaragua (24)	+18	—4	?2	Bishops (2)		—2	
USA (22)	+9	—13		Priests (24)	+13	—11	
Brazil (4)	+4			Sisters (31)	+24	—5	?2
Mexico (4)	+3	—1		Deacons (2)	+2		
Santo Domingo (2)	+2						
Colombia (1)	+1						
Canada (1)	+1						
UK (1)	+1						

Parroquia Cristo Redentor
Muelle de los Bueyes
("Ox-ford")
Nicaragua
29 July 1986

Dear Friends,

Thank God Nicaraguans have a sense of humor. It may stand them in good stead when the US Marines come ashore for the umpteenth time in their history. A few weeks ago I was travelling on horseback through some of the worst mud swamplands in this rural parish. Only ten years ago it had been tropical rain-forest, but the trees had been cut down by a hard-working, if partly misguided, farmer, who hoped to rear cattle in the cleared space. Perhaps a herd of African hippopotami might, within a few generations, have adapted to the ubiquitous mud, but no known breed of cattle stood the remotest chance. However, the farmer was not beaten. I rode (or rather, plunged) past an extraordinary confusion of timber and palm-branches that must have been the farmhouse, and noticed that he had painted boldly across the doorway: The name of this farm is 'BETTER THAN NOTHING'.

And I suppose it was. It sustains him and his family. He is certainly safe from attack (the contras would be worse off than Napoleon retreating from Moscow if they ever got embedded in his horrific swamps).

'Better than Nothing' seems to me a good description of Nicaragua in the last month or so. On June 25 we heard the dreaded news that Washington had approved the $100 million, and had thrown in an extra $10 million, to help the mercenary contras destroy the freely elected government of this country. In my parish, people filled the village churches in a spontaneous gesture of prayer. Others filled the taverns instead. Many of us did both. Two days later we were rewarded with a compensation prize (better than nothing): the International Court at The Hague, after investigations lasting more than two years, pronounced the US Government an unjust aggressor in the war against Nicaragua. Predictably, the Reagan administration rejected the verdict, but perhaps the rest of the world, and history, will not.

Nobody here was surprised when the Sandinistas reacted to the American belligerence. The expulsion of Bishop Vega 'until the end of the US aggression' is inexplicable only to those unaware of his notoriously frequent trips to Washington where he constantly denounced the Sandinista Government and encouraged the giving of money to the contras. After 15 years as bishop of a well-populated diocese he has only eight priests, all of them foreigners, all of them over 55 years of age. Better than nothing?

On 3 July, 32 civilians—mostly women and children—were blown up and killed in Bocaycito by a contra road mine. The same day the passenger boat from Rama to Bluefields (our provincial capital) was attacked; one woman was killed and seven people were injured.

It pains me to see my parishioners eating less than they ate last year. With less rice and fewer beans on each plate, there is embarrassment at the arrival of an unexpected friend or relation. The war effort is producing under-nourishment.

In my weaker moments I am tempted to organise soup kitchens. Many priests do that sort of thing in different parts of the world. Certain readers of these letters might then be relieved that I had stopped 'being political'. But I know this would be wrong. The problem in Nicaragua is political, caused by political interference from the most powerful country in the world. If the whole of the Central American region were allowed to choose its own political culture, without hindrance and pressures, these people would be among the best-fed in the world. I intend, therefore, to stand by these Nicaraguan farm-workers, and to make known the justice of their cause.

God is not a Lord of death and war, nor a defender of the 'status quo' in a world where the status of two-thirds of the people is inhuman. I feel sure that life for these people is meant to be a *lot* better than nothing.

God bless you,

Padre Juan Luis (Medcalf)

Casa de la Cultura
Cara de Mono
("Monkey Face")
Zelaya Central
Nicaragua
12 October 1986

Dear Friends,

The streetgames of small children provide, in my experience, a reflection of the priorities and problems of their countries. When I worked in a shanty-town of Lima, the favourite game was 'borrachitos'—drunken fathers and enraged mothers, acted out in a scenario worthy of Dickens, and with a realism reminiscent of Chaplin. This Peruvian street game reflected the massive unemployment and the despondency common to most Third World countries.

Here in Nicaragua children play war-games. They make tanks and planes out of mud. When shot down by imaginary bullets they twist and writhe in simulated pain before falling dead. Contras and Sandinistas instead of Cowboys and Indians.

On returning to this rural parish after a three-week break in Britain, I was struck by the overwhelming proportion of children and youths. Half the population of Nicaragua is under fifteen. Most of the cabinet ministers are in their thirties and forties. I don't recollect meeting a schoolteacher over 35.

Last week's national hero was a 19-year old soldier with only five months military service. He shot down a US military plane carrying three American veterans from the Vietnam war and a large quantity of arms destined for the contras. If the elation caused by this 'slip of a lad' (as the Irish would call him) is anything to go by, the American Marines will be in for a very rough passage if they are ever sent in to subdue this country.

Closer to home, my colleague Fr. José Curcio is helping a 12-year old girl with elephantiasis in one leg. This terrible deformation, fairly common in tropical countries, requires the sort of surgery that is not yet available in Nicaragua. Fortunately, friends in Canada have rallied round to pay for an operation in a Toronto hospital.

In the village of Cara de Mono there were three deaths in September. All of them were young people. Segundino Torres, 24, was captured, tortured horribly and killed by the contras. His mother, who sells beer and cigarettes, wept quietly during the Requiem mass I said two days ago.

Yolanda, 19, was a child prostitute under the Somoza dictatorship. With the Sandinista Revolution she was 'rehabilitated', joined the army and died on September 24 in circumstances still unexplained. Her mother spends most of her time looking after a son who is 'loco', a mental defective.

Julito, 11, died when he was fishing in the River Mico. A tropical storm caused a tree to fall on him, killing him instantly. His school-mates attended a memorial service last Wednesday.

Meanwhile, my colleagues Jorge and Paddy have been in Los Laureles, organising a *Semana de la Cultura* (Culture Week — how awful it sounds in English!) The children of the village were spellbound as they learned to paint with natural colours squeezed out of flowers. Today they will present a concert of local dances, songs, and sketches for their parents and others belonging to the minority world of adults. War-games will be down-graded for a day or so, perhaps.

One of the points about the David and Goliath story is that the Philistine giant—possessed of maturity, strength and arrogant self-confidence—was challenged by a mere 'slip of a lad'. Nicaragua may seem to outsiders a mere slip of a country; to those of us privileged to live here this is no bad thing. Gaudeamus igitur...

Affectionately

Padre Juan (Medcalf)

Parroquia Cristo Redentor
Muelle de los Bueyes
("Ox-ford")
Zelaya Central
Nicaragua

7 November 1986

Dear Friends,

November in Nicaragua means trees full of ripe oranges, lemons and grapefruit. We find our breakfast under the trees each morning. Before this citrus harvest we had had three months of bananas and breadfruit, and before it was mostly coconuts (in fact I had a recurrent dream in May and June that I was about to be killed by a ripe coconut falling accurately and forcefully on my head!).

There are many other tropical fruits eaten by my parishioners here in Central Zelaya. When at last peace comes the survivors will inhabit a Garden of Eden.

In the meantime the maiming, the killing and the enforced recruitment have all increased. On October 14 a civilian bus was ambushed by the contras on its way to Muelle de los Bueyes. One of our catechists was on board. Three civilians (two women and an old man), a Sandinista soldier and two contras were killed in the skirmish. The contras took four hostages, including the bus driver. Just five days ago I travelled on the same bus and chatted to the same driver, happily back in his old job after a forced march in torrential storms through the rain-forests of Central Zelaya. Although he had not been tortured, there was a glazed look on his face, similar perhaps to that of any other Lazarus called back unexpectedly to a new lease of life.

On October 15, the day after the ambush of the bus, two Sandinista officers were shot dead while riding a motorbike between Muelle and Cara de Mono.

On October 26, in the village of Tamalera (four hours by horseback from Muelle) the *campesinos* (peasant farmers) were assembled in the Catholic chapel for their weekly 'Celebration of the Word'. A group of armed contras burst into the chapel. Using threats and physical violence, they took away nine young men against their will for what must be presumed to be military recruitment. No regard was paid to the protests of parents and relations. We heard that two of the nine have managed to escape and return to Tamalera.

In spite of increased violence on the road linking the Atlantic and Pacific oceans, newspapers and letters have been getting through to us without too much delay. For over a month now the chief news item in the Managua dailies has been the trial of US pilot Eugene Hasenfus, sole survivor of a C-123 aircraft carrying military hardware to the contras, shot down on October 5 by a portable ground-to-air missile. Whatever the eventual outcome (the present government has abolished the death penalty and has established 30 years as the maximum jail sentence) there is great interest in the trial.

I was intrigued by a notebook belonging to Hasenfus, which revealed the code names used by the contras in their squalid little war against Nicaragua; the daily newspapers published a few examples:

U.S.A. = PLAYBOY
WASHINGTON = TOP FLOOR
RIFLES = APPLES
EXPLOSIVES = PEARS

So the Playboy on the Top Floor is kindly despatching more planeloads of apples and pears to a country (code name NICKERS perhaps?) whose people desperately want peace, a country where oranges and bananas and passion-fruit are not military code names for destruction, but real food and drink — for life!

Affectionately,
Padre Juan Luis Medcalf

Parroquia Cristo Redentor
Muelle de los Bueyes
("Ox-ford")
Nicaragua

12 December 1986

Dear Friends,

The greater part of this parish is a political no man's land. Once I leave the heavily-guarded highroad uniting the Atlantic and Pacific oceans, it is as if I had entered a different country.

This vast hinterland of what was once tropical rainforest is divided into *comarcas* or regions. We have over fifty *comarcas* in our parish, and I have recently spent a lot of time visiting them on horseback. A typical *comarca* would have thirty or forty farmsteads, spread out over the hills, with at least a kilometer of rough, muddy track between each wooden hut. The only public building would be the Catholic chapel, though sometimes there is an evangelical chapel as well.

Fortunately, I have not yet met the contras, though it seems they are aware of my movements, and they are never far away. As I ride beside my *baquiano*, or local guide, there is plenty to help me forget the agony of the war. The very names of the *comarcas* are suggestive enough — *Painted Rocks, Turkey-Hens, Black Hat (Sombrero Negro), Conformity, Edible Iguana, Wild Bee Hive* and *Boiled Corn-meal* were some of the regions I visited in November and December.

The Delegate of the Word of God in Las Pavas *(The Turkey-Hens)* gave me a great welcome to his community on November 13. Forty-five-year old Zacarias Garzón had persuaded almost every family to attend the 24-hour mission I was to direct in the chapel that had formerly served also as a school until the contras abducted the teacher. He introduced me as the only 'sacerdote ingles' working in Nicaragua, and jocularly reminded his fellow farmers that most of the Englishmen who had visited the Caribbean in the past had been pirates looking for Spanish gold. In my reply I thanked Zacarías and his villagers on behalf of all turkey-eating Britons, for Central America's gift to the world, and suggested that the turkeys after which their village had been named had brought more pleasure to Britain than the Spanish gold. There followed many hours of baptisms, weddings, confessions, first communions, and question-and-answer sermons. I remember particularly how, well past sundown, the young men of that com-

munity debated with me the precise meaning of the commandment 'Thou shalt not kill'. Zacarías seemed content (a premonition perhaps?) to direct the debate without proffering an opinion of his own.

Three weeks later, on December 2, the contras dragged Zacarías Garzón from his hut and slit his throat in the nearby forest. I heard the news yesterday.

Why Zacarías? He was not known to be a Sandinista supporter. (Nobody in Nicaragua's no-man's-land makes known his political allegiance, except in the secrecy of the confessional.) One of his nephews, it is true, works for the Ministry of Agriculture. Perhaps the contras are afraid of strong leadership.

There is so much more that has happened in Nicaragua that is more dramatic — bridges have been blown up, more teachers raped and abducted, border villages strafed by US fighterplanes. Here in Muelle de los Bueyes villagers are opening up their homes to war orphans, even though they could be made targets of contra reprisals for doing so.

But for me, Zacarías is more real. I know that he was prepared for death. Those who knew him will treasure the memory of a courageous leader. He joins a long roll of heroes and martyrs in Central America's struggle for independence and dignity.

May Christmas and the New Year bring us all an increased hope, and lasting peace.

Padre Juan Luis
(John Medcalf)

1987

Parroquia Cristo Redentor
Muelle de los Bueyes
("Ox-ford")
Zelaya Central
Nicaragua

5 January 1987

Dear Friends,

Four weeks without a single killing must be a record for this Nicaraguan parish. A week or so before Christmas I thought I heard the familiar rat-tat-tat of guns in the distance, but it turned out to be a Dendrocopos villosus (a Hairy Woodpecker, known here as a carpintero) noisily carving its nest in a mango tree. In fact, the only real machine-guns we heard in December were fired by Sandinista soldiers after the Midnight mass, to celebrate the birthday of Christ.

The highlight of the month for our Rural Libraries team was the celebration of a Christmas Festival on December 20. We had been asked by the local Sandinistas to organize 'a religious-cultural fiesta which would include Catholics and Protestants and anybody else who wants to come along'. The result was a 6-hour marathon of village Nativity plays from 15 different regions. There was no element of competition, and no attempt at politicking. We were almost embarrassed by the enormous, unsophisticated delight of hundreds of Nicaraguan families as they watched endless shepherds swathed in sheets trooping across the stage, and innumerable actors and actresses making their theatrical debuts as the front halves of donkeys or the rear halves of oxen. The happiest man of the day, I think, was the Sandinista mayor of Rama, a deeply religious man who in recent years had been cold-shouldered by a conservative priest for his political affiliation.

Three days later, on December 23, Father Miguel D'Escoto (the Chancellor, or Foreign Minister) held a Christmas party in his back garden. Priests and nuns who had joined him on last February's Way of the Cross were invited, but only about fifty of us could make the appointment. While we ate a simple meal of boiled beef, rice and beans, the Nicaraguan President Daniel Ortega joined us. He stayed for more than two hours. We sat

in a circle and he invited us to put questions. 'Compañero Daniel', as he is addressed, is a slightly-built 39-year old, with no natural gift for oratory, and to whom smiles do not come easily. The years in prison and the physical torture administered by Somoza's National Guard have left their imprint. Yet the untheatrical simplicity of the man is his greatest asset.

He answered all our questions without evasion, and with a remarkable intellectual command of a broad range of subjects. 1986 had been a difficult year for the Nicaraguan economy, but the Hague International Court's verdict against US aggression was an important victory. The contras had failed to win the support of the civilian population. In spite of massive American funding they had not captured even the smallest village inside Nicaragua's territorial limits.

The church news was also good. The Pope had changed his ambassador (or nuncio) in Managua, and the hard-line bishops were beginning to listen to world opinion and to the less affluent among their flocks.

The President sadly remarked that for some people the Nicaraguan government was incapable of any good action. When Eugene Hasenfus, the American pilot captured while taking bullets and bombs to the contras, was given a 30-year jail sentence in November, President Reagan called the verdict 'inhuman'. When the same pilot was given a pardon a week before Christmas, the act was dismissed as 'a propagandistic trick.'

The Christmas Eve celebrations in the 60 villages that make up this parish were mercifully unmarked by contra activity. In many places the religious ceremonies were followed by community meals of tortilla and rice.

Several villages on the main road had a circus to entertain them over the Christmas holidays. I went to a performance in Cara de Mono. A few dozen wooden planks were arranged like a cock-pit or miniature amphitheatre, and the whole precarious structure was surrounded with sugar-bag sacking to lend an air of privacy to the evening. The entire circus troupe consisted of a family of five and their monkey. The father threw long-handled knives at his teenage daughter while a four-year old son heightened the tension with a series of drum-rolls on an empty dried-milk tin. An eight-year old girl played the 'smart kid' to offset her father's clowning antics; her fast repartee stole the show. The monkey seemed to be out of sorts that night, and refused to do anything except shake its fists at the public. The clown's wife was absent, but her husband promised that she would play the star role the following evening in a horrific and blood-curdling drama called 'Frankenstein's Castle.' Minds and imaginations boggled. There was no vulgarity in the entertainment (perhaps because the priest was in the front row!) and the only political joke was about the world's biggest clown living in the White House.

May his clowning in 1987 allow these poor people to live.

Sincerely,

Padre Juan Luis Medcalf

Parroquia Catolica
Muelle de los Bueyes
("Ox-ford")
Zelaya Central
Nicaragua

12 February 1987

Dear Friends,

When I write these letters from Nicaragua I sometimes worry whether I am giving a balanced presentation. This war is like a huge, garishly-painted backcloth on a theatre stage — always seen by the spectators, but not necessarily by the actors. We here can turn our backs and forget for a while. I can perform marriages, and christen the resultant babies; people can laugh and sing and enjoy a visiting circus. But it's not natural to have your back turned all the time, and the closeness of it all is horrifying.

I visited the village of Boca Azul *(Blue Mouth)* in mid-January. A greener, lusher corner of tropical rain-forest is difficult to imagine. Howler monkeys and macaws competed to drown the hymn-singing! Some five or six years ago, shortly before the war began, several villagers decided to construct their wooden, palm-thatched huts close together, by the riverside. A very sensible idea, especially for the women and children, who normally live in very isolated conditions. The sight now is pitiful — charred timbers are all that remain of this settlement. Only the chapel was spared by the contras in a hit-and-run raid a year ago. Most of the villagers managed to hide in the forest until the terrorists ('freedom fighters' according to Washington) had left.

A trip to Rio Plata on January 24 was, on the other hand, pure pleasure. The villagers have organized themselves into a cooperative, and most of the land is jointly owned. These families were really proud of their achievement. They produce coffee, bananas, oranges, beans and maize on the common land, and onions and tomatoes on their own private plots. The government helps them in all sorts of ways, but there seems to be no heavy-handed interference. They have a successful primary school, and the children had even heard of Rochdale, where the first cooperative saw the light of day. I felt proud of my British passport in Rio Plata.

This is the sort of thing that can only happen when a village is well defended from contra violence, and it is the sort of thing that is, I suppose, the real reason for the war — the threat of a good example, sending shivers down the spines of despotic or reactionary governments in other countries.

Last weekend, three young men were killed by the contras in different sectors of this parish. I performed the burial of the last of these, 17-year old Armando, from Cara de Mono village. I had known him very well. He and his three best friends had volunteered for military service last September, before they had reached the minimum age. News reached the village that one of the four had been killed, and only later was the name obtained. The suffering undergone by families and friends can be imagined. Yesterday I learned that near Presilla village the contras compelled a youth to hold his older brother's head while that head was hacked off with a machete. The younger brother was then freed to tell the tale.

All this is part of the horrific backcloth of war, against which my parishioners try to survive and not fall prey to despair. I tell them that I believe in ultimate victory, that God is on the side of the downtrodden. I go further with some of the leaders, and tell them that I believe the war will end when the North Americans change their President. Should I go further, and encourage them to enlist in the Sandinista army, knowing the risks for themselves and their families? To be completely silent on the question is an evasion of reality, a turning away from the backcloth of blood and sacrifice.

I have had two more reasons to be proud of my country of birth. In January three members of a coffee-picking brigade from Southern England called in to share with me their experiences and insights. Then a group of eight building-workers from Nottingham arrived in nearby Juigalpa to build a factory for roof-tiles in three months. The idealism and effort of these young people are part of the heroic struggle for Nicaragua's independence. They, too, are part of the backcloth, along with the blood and the pain.

With affection and solidarity,

Padre Juan Luis Medcalf

Parroquia Catolica
Muelle de los Bueyes
("Ox-ford")
Zelaya Central
Nicaragua
9 March 1987

Dear Friends,

There are many ways of being killed in Nicaragua, but I had forgotten that people could be killed with kindness. On 1 March I paid my monthly visit to Red Diamond, the most eastern of the sixty villages that make up this parish.

'Doña Rosa is dying and needs the last sacraments,' I was told. So I set out. I had not, however, imagined that fifty villagers would accompany me! On arrival, an hour later, the dying woman was hugged, kissed, blessed and caressed by each person in turn. Small gifts of rice and beans were left in dark corners of the small hut, assurances of prayers were given and received, and promises made to return with still more villagers once the monthly mass was concluded.

I have not heard any more of Doña Rosa's fate, but most probably she is now dead, killed with kindness.

Three weeks ago we inaugurated our largest Rural Library to date, in the village of Los Laureles. This village has been harder hit by contra terrorism than any other in this area. There have been at least ten civilian deaths in five years, most of them church leaders and members of rural cooperatives. Since there are only a few dozen families in The Laurels, the proportion of those killed is high. All the more reason to enjoy watching the young children reading coloured story albums, and seeing their parents fascinated by books like *Where There Is No Doctor* and *Accountancy Without Tears*.

The Nicaraguan war has certainly not extinguished hope and acts of kindness. In fact, it has probably caused their increase.

The problems faced by our peasant farmers are very different from those of their city cousins. The chief preoccupation here is with the capacity of the soil to feed the families who live and work on it. About 80% of my parishioners own their individual plot of land, about 10% are members of land cooperatives, and the rest are landless refugees from remote war zones. The cooperatives, where between 15 and 30 families own and work a tract of land, are undoubtedly a feather in the cap of the Sandinista government. Their formation was made easier by the fact that the Somoza family, during the 40-year long dictatorship, had made themselves owners of one-fifth of Nicaragua's cultivable land. This was all confiscated and used as the basis of the new cooperatives. If anything, the government is overdoing the perks to these privileged peasant farmers. There is a danger of killing with kindness. Yet I have to admit that only in the cooperatives is there any attempt to control the wholesale destruction of the rain forests or the will to do something about soil erosion. Land tenure is perhaps the most urgent problem in the entire Third World, which is why the Nicaraguan experiments must be allowed to survive.

At night-time, lying in hammocks strung up on moonlit mahogany verandas, farmers tell me stories of large pig-like animals called *dantos* (tapirs), exotic long-tailed birds called quetzals, and innumerable varieties of trees formerly exported as timber to the US. All are now in imminent danger of extinction.

Unfortunately the people best able to protect our ecology are themselves the targets of killers. On February 17, the contras burned all the houses of the Rio Rama cooperative, killing seven and wounding twenty men, women and children. On March 5, the Fernando Salazar cooperative was attacked, with five dead.

Just three nights ago I was nearly blown out of my hammock by two bomb-blasts in the village of Presilla. The only real casualties were the electricity pylons and our nervous systems. The following night, March 7, I was back in Muelle de los Bueyes, just in time to witness the first ever direct attack on this strategically-placed village. As in Presilla, the Sandinista militia responded promptly and effectively. The only visible results of the contra attack are a badly-damaged house, two young women severely wounded by shrapnel, and a grim determination on the faces of villagers to resist what may be the beginning of a desperate last-ditch attempt to set up a provisional 'puppet' government here in Central Zelaya.

The official slogan this year is *Aquí No Se Rinde Nadie* — 'Nobody is Surrendering Over Here'. It would be wonderful if people were only killed with kindness.

Affectionately,

Padre Juan Luis
(John Medcalf)

Parroquia Cristo Redentor
Muelle de los Bueyes
("Ox-ford")
Zelaya Central
Nicaragua

13 April 1987

Dear Friends,

People here become very passionate about the reasons for the chronic shortage of almost everything. A few Sundays ago, while saying mass in the village of Red Diamond, I quoted the following true story in order to encourage the pews to speak back. Two church leaders in another village had been selling their cheese and milk on the black market instead of using the official channels. As a result, they have both become quite wealthy by Nicaraguan standards, and apparently see nothing wrong in their conduct.

The story unleashed a flood of comments, all of them highly critical of black marketeers, speculators and hoarders, especially those who take advantage of wartime shortages. The term 'religious hypocrite' was bandied about. One of several Sandinista soldiers attending mass raised the only laugh of the morning when he said that the priest was now an accessory after the fact, and guilty of breaking the law if he failed to denounce the two criminals. I felt relieved that they had all laughed.

The following Sunday I related the same incident in Muelle de los Bueyes and was confronted with a hostile silence followed by a tidal wave of interventions criticizing bureaucracy, government incompetence, and the lack of a free market economy. Nobody in Muelle that morning was in a mood to raise a laugh in order to lower the temperature!

Two villages with entirely opposed reactions to a matter that closely concerns their survival. Red Diamond peple are poor farmers who have benefited from the 1979 Revolution, and give it their support. Oxford people are mostly shopkeepers presiding over empty shelves; they are not very sympathetic to a government that controls their profits. Strangely perhaps, even most Oxford tradesmen would agree with the Red Diamond farmers that the *chief* culprit for their present calamitous situation is the President of the USA.

The sun, during these months, is Public Enemy No. 2. The only wildlife that revels in the suffocating heat are the cicadas — green hoppers, the size and shape of a fat thumb; their high-pitched monotone as unmusical as the wind in the telegraph wires. All other living things seem to sleep through the cicadas' daytime din and wake up when the sun has finished doing its damage. Not long ago I was half asleep myself, on a mule returning at midday from San Isidro village, when I sighted a keel-billed toucan sitting on a branch a few feet above me, its eyes and huge beak firmly shut. I wondered whether it was dreaming of a pint of Guinness!

Unfortunately, the temperature of the war has also crept up in the last month. Of six villages I visited in the last week of March, only one was not mourning a recent death. On March 25, a few hours after I had left the dirt road near the well-defended village of San Martín, the contras ambushed two vehicles, killing ten civilians and gravely wounding a young mother. Ironically, the previous day I had been asked to preside at a service of thanksgiving in San Martín for eight National Servicemen who had just been demobilized after two years of fighting. They sat in the front benches of the chapel, a little self-conscious in their new civilian clothes, the objects of admiring side-glances from grateful mothers and marriageable girls in flowered dresses. I tried to lower the temperature by telling a ridiculous story about an elderly farmer who refused to kneel down during the consecration of the bread and wine. The equally elderly priest called out sharply —

— What's making you rebellious today, Don Carlos?
El capitalismo or *el comunismo?*

— Neither, Padre . . . just *el reumatismo.*

Two of these new civilians were among the ten killed the following day. I wish now that I had been less frivolous.

'Do you think the *gringo* will invade Nicaragua?' is the question I am asked most frequently. Sometimes I think a short, sharp battle would be the lesser evil, instead of the prolonged agony called politely 'low intensity warfare.'

Easter is only a few days ahead. I am certain that these brave, long-suffering people will find a message of hope and new life with which to support each other. They will find strength to put up with the rationing and the shortages, and even the daily killings at the hands of the mercenaries. They know that the sun can only scorch the earth for so many months in the year before the rains pour down and make life green again.

Happy Easter!

Padre Juan Luis Medcalf

May 7, 1987

In May 1987 Fr. Medcalf was unable to write his usual monthly letter. Instead his friends received the following article.

If God had stood as candidate for president in the Nicaraguan elections two and a half years ago, he would have romped home. As it turned out, all the candidates, not least the successful Sandinista, Daniel Ortega, were careful to recognize the high popularity ratings given by most of the three million Nicaraguans to God and to the religions organized in his name.

One of the state radio stations begins its daily broadcasting with a well known religious song composed by the country's foremost composer and singer, Carlos Mejía Godoy. The music is allegro con brio (with faint memories of 'How Much is that Doggie in the Window?'). The text is unashamedly liberation theology:

> You are the God of the poor, the God who is human and simple, the God who perspires in the market, the God with a face that is wrinkled.
>
> This is why I can talk to you plainly and speak with the words of my people, for you are God-become-worker, for you are the Carpenter-Christ.

As a parish priest working in a rural part of Nicaragua, I frequently compare the faith and religious practice of my cattle-rearing parishioners with the beliefs of their contemporaries in other countries. Many of my questions remain only partially answered.

Nicaragua shares with the other Hispano-American republics the inheritance of a Christianity mostly Roman Catholic in allegiance. The Spanish Catholicism of the sixteenth century, the century of the conquistadores, was marked by two characteristics.

The first was peculiarly Hispanic, since it derived from the final defeat of the Moors in 1492 under the leadership of the monarchs Ferdinand and Isabel. In the same year of grace 'Columbus crossed the ocean blue,' bearing with him to the New World a triumphant Spanish Catholicism in which cross and sword were as inextricably united as the monarchs of Spain. To this day, in the Andean villages of Bolivia and Peru, the most popular saint is often Santiago Matamoros (St. James the Moor-killer), arrogantly depicted astride a horse, Toledo sword in hand, while underneath the horse the writhing bodies of unfortunate infidels give mute witness to God's partiality for the conquistadores.

The second inspiration of New World Catholicism was the Counter-Reformation of the sixteenth century. The Council of Trent was the occasion for emphasising those doctrines and practices denied by the Reformers, but the long and hazardous ocean journeys from Spain delayed an orthodox enactment of the Council Fathers' decrees. Mariolatry, hagiolatry, clericalization, liturgical and biblical fossilization were integral ingredients of the Good News imparted to the indigenous Americans.

On the positive side, the Spanish Inquisition drew a blank in the New World. After all, you could accuse Atahualpa and Montezuma of being 'infidels', and therefore worthy of defeat and death in the tradition of the Muslim Moors, but heresy was outside their ken. However, the Spanish province of the Order of Preachers (the Dominicans) produced in Fray Bartolomé de las Casas a *defensor indiorum* whose compassion for the exploited Amerindians would be remembered tenderly in the centuries ahead. He, rather than Torquemada, is the most lasting monument to the Dominican Order in the Americas.

The monuments left by the Jesuits in South America are now mostly covered with Paraguayan jungle creepers, and have recently been brought to the attention of cinema-goers in 'The Mission'. The Jesuit experiments in theocracy have been for Latin American Christians rather what the Arthurian legends were for medieval and Victorian Englishmen.

Nicaragua inherited from Spain the fusion of sword and cross. The country is named after the Indian chief Nicarao who did a dubious deal with the conquistadores, culminating in the handing over of large tracts of lands as well as in his own baptism.

The third Bishop of Nicaragua, Antonio de Valdivieso, was butchered in 1550 by the Toledo swords he had valiantly denounced. Today a very successful ecumenical centre named after the martyred prelate operates in Managua. It is headed by a Franciscan priest and is constantly denounced by the present-day bishops, the successors to Valdivieso.

If God was not actually absent from Nicaragua in the seventeenth and eighteenth centuries, he was at least strangely silent in the corridors or patios of power. Governed in theory from Guatemala City, the country became effectively divided into two parts — the Pacific coastlands, where the Spanish-Indian cross-fertilization became more *cafe au lait* with each generation, and the Atlantic coastlands, where British buccaneers carved off slivers of the jungle and gave beads to the natives, so as to ensure a friendly harbour or two in between their Caribbean adventures. It was not until 1894 that President Zelaya finally obtained the Atlantic provinces (which now bear his name) from the British Crown.

President Zelaya also legitimized the presence of non-Roman Catholic churches in Nicaragua. Anglican and Moravian missions had been established in the Atlantic zone during the nineteenth century, and their influence on the language and culture of the Misquito Indians remains as strong today as it was a hundred years ago. In 1985, I attended an Anglican Eucharist in Managua. Apart from a couple of white ladies with floppy hats who might have dropped in on an exchange visit from Leamington Spa, the entire congregation of about sixty was black. The officiating priest made no reference, either in his homily or his prayers, to the escalating war and the grave consequences for the Nicaraguan population. He followed Eucharistic Canon No. 3 from the *Missale Romanum.* Perhaps he was acclimatizing himself for Leamington Spa.

What I glimpsed in St. George's Anglican church, Managua, I have since seen repeated in many Roman Catholic churches up and down the country. God is as popular as ever. Church attendance, however, is not what it was.

There is one exception: the fast-growing evangelical sects of North American parentage. Charismatic in their worship, fundamentalist in their biblical beliefs, they are also arrogantly right-wing in their political ideology. Their God is the champion of unbridled capitalism and US hegemony, at least in the western hemisphere. Their Devil is very much alive and kicking, and seems to travel frequently between Moscow, Havana and Vatican City. Roman Catholicism is, for these sects, the Scarlet Woman of the Apocalypse, and it is no coincidence that red is also the favoured colour of the Kremlin. Heaven knows what John Paul II makes of such an unlikely cocktail.

It is difficult to imagine the future of 'The Church of the Prophecy', 'The Church of the Word' and 'The Evangelical Church of Central America', to name but three of these fashionable sects. They began life with two great advantages: the deep religious feelings of the majority of Nicaraguans, and an apocalyptic situation of violence and war where any trumped-up messiah is assured of a hearing. They are characterized by an enthusiasm in the original sense of that word, 'in God', redolent of Calvin's city-state of Geneva and the other 'enthusiasms' described by the late Monsignor Ronald Knox in his book of that title.

The mainstream of Roman Catholicism continues to be, for most Nicaraguans, the normal ambience of their faith. I am frequently surprised by the sense of catholicity in my rural parishioners, whose world in every other respect is circumscribed by the nearest river or the chain of forested hills where the next cattle ranch begins. Bishops and priests may be remote, but the present Pope is very real, especially since his visit to Nicaragua in 1983.

God, however, is much more real than the Pope, and rather more human as well. The Nicaraguan God has some delightful characteristics, among which is a sense of humour reminiscent of Chaucer and Kipling. On one occasion I was travelling on horseback through the tropical rain forests with a deacon as my guide. We were suddenly confronted with a dozen or so howler monkeys swinging in the trees just above us, howling in horrific chorus with voices that might have been the result of cross-breeding between a donkey and a lioness. The visual effect however was even more remarkable. The male howler monkey (and they all appeared to be males) is completely black except for its testicles, which are, in startling contrast, snowy white. The deacon, once the surprise encounter was over, entertained me with the following narration.

> Once upon a time, when the whole of Nicaragua was a jungle, God decided to hold a music festival for all the animals and birds. It took place in the tops of the giant cedar trees near the ocean where the sun rises. The musical contributions were extremely varied, from the gentle sounds of the humming-bird to the squawking of the great macaw, and the chattering of the green-and-red parrots. The last competitors of all were the howler monkeys. In those far-off days all the howler monkeys were completely white, without a hint of any other shade or colour. But when they struck up their infernal howling from the tops of the giant cedar trees even God stopped up his ears in horror. Since the howler monkeys failed to take the hint and continued with their ear-splitting noise, God began sending thunder-caps to shut them up, but to no effect. So God then sent down streaks of lightning to the tops of the giant cedar trees, and the howler monkeys were so frightened that they instinctively covered up their private parts to protect them from burning. From that

day on, all howler monkeys are the colour of charcoal from top to bottom—with a small exception in the middle.

God is part of day-to-day conversation. *Dios primero* (God comes first) is not so much a puritanical brake on some pleasurable activity as a reminder that life has its priorities. 'Thanks be to God and the Revolution' peppers the parlance of the two-thirds of the population that supports the Sandinista 'process'.' Even the use of the simple word *Adios* gives the impression that its meaning, 'God be with you', is really intended, rather than the neutral significance of the English contraction of the same phrase, 'good-bye'.

Sacramental practice varies greatly. Infant baptism is a *sine qua non* of social life, though unbaptized babies are not known in Nicaragua as *moritos* (little Moors) as in many other parts of Hispano-America. There is a difference of opinion about the age for confirmation. The Atlantic Coast bishops (Capuchin Franciscans from Wisconsin) favour 15 as the minimum age, whereas the other eight dioceses of the country insist on seven to eight as the ideal.

Although many Nicaraguan males find monogamy burdensome, and indefensible in an under-populated country, there is probably rather more fidelity and less adultery than in most Western countries. Strangely, this is not reflected in the number of 'church' or 'civil' marriages. In this parish of approximately thirty thousand people, we celebrated only 27 church weddings in 1985. The recruitment of so many young men for the defense of the country has some bearing on the low numbers, but it does not provide the entire answer. Celibacy is admired from a distance, but not readily imitated; something like half the priests and nuns working here are foreign-born.

Sickness and death find the Nicaraguans at their best. I once had the good fortune to faint in an overcrowded bus (all buses are overcrowded). Within seconds I was given the best seat near an open window, and became the object of a vast process of fanning in which every passenger, as well as the conductor, seemed to participate. Assorted liquids were poured down my throat, and the bus driver would have made a special detour to a hospital had I not protested that I was by then fully recovered and extremely comfortable.

The dying and the dead are always accompanied by large numbers of friends, relations and neighbours. The village 'wakes' frequently go on for 24 hours, punctuated with the praying of the rosary, the reading of bible passages, hymn-singing and the dispensing of refreshments at public cost (a collection is made among the neighbours). On All Souls' Day wreaths of multi-coloured plastic flowers are taken to the cemeteries and placed on the graves of relations and friends. The heavy toll of the present war means that wakes are all too frequent, and floristry is a flourishing concern.

It is sometimes observed by outsiders that all the poets, musicians, theologians and artists are on the side of the Nicaraguan Revolution. Most of the bishops, on the other hand, are against it. Perhaps the saving grace of Nicaraguan Christians is that they have never expected too much of their prelates. They have had one martyred bishop, and another (during the First World war) who strongly denounced US bullying. There was once an Argentine bishop who adopted as his motto 'One eye on the Scriptures, the other on the poor'.' He was killed, in 1976, for his bifocal philosophy, which had led him inevitably to denounce the barbarity of Videla's military junta. We are not all of the stuff that martyrs are made of.

The 'God of the poor' lives on in the tropical rain forests and the shabby shanty towns of Nicaragua. He may well, under a different theology, exist also in the air-conditioned limousines of Cardinal Miguel Obando y Bravo, but I imagine He feels uncomfortable.

John Medcalf
Caro de Mono
Nicaragua

Parroquia Catolica
Muelle de los Bueyes
("Ox-ford")
Zelaya Central
Nicaragua

17 June 1987

Dear Friends,

At last I have met the contras face to face. It was bound to happen sooner or later, and it happened last Wednesday, June 10. I had been visiting the villages on the north side of the only paved road in this parish. The first rains of the year had put an end to the paralyzing heat that had lasted nearly four months, and I was lucky to have a marvellous native guide, or *baquiano,* called Balbino, who could recognise all the sounds of the forest and had an eye for unusual animal tracks. There had been great excitement a week ago, he told me, because a *tapir* had been hunted and killed close to where we were. This missing link between the wild pig and the elephant had not been seen for several years and was thought to have vanished completely from our area. We tied our mules to a thick creeper and plunged further into the forest. Balbino's dog ran ahead and chased a colony of about a dozen raccoons up into a silk-cotton tree; they hissed and spat at us from low-lying branches. There was more excitement when the *baquiano* discovered the fresh imprints of 'a large cat', possibly a lynx or even a jaguar.

It was the following afternoon, as we rounded a hill called Campana (because it is bell-shaped), that we ran into our first contras. They must have been watching us from the hill-top as we rode in their direction. Four men dressed in green-and-black camouflage detained us briefly without speaking, then waved us both on towards a nearby farmhouse. Some 50 yards before arriving we suddenly found ourselves surrounded by a company of about 40 soldiers whose average age I guessed to be 17 or 18 years. One of them held up a bible and a rosary, but none of them spoke until an older man, who must have been their commanding officer, strode up with an outstretched hand which I took limply, without enthusiasm.

He spoke with a deference that was almost fawning. They were fighting to save their country from an atheistic dictatorship. Nobody desired peace more than these loyal sons of the Catholic church. Their victory against the Soviet Sandinistas was inevitable, etc., etc.

I remained seated on my mule, uncomfortably aware that my every gesture and expression was being carefully observed, and that they were all waiting for me to say something. The slightest word of encouragement would have elicited wild cheering, I felt.

Looking back, I wish I had been more courageous. I told them that the Sandinista soldiers were also Catholics, were also fighting for their country, were also longing for an end to the war. I told them to listen carefully to the voice of their individual conscience, which was far more important than the voice of any *jefe* they might have to obey. I suppose the general coldness of my tone, rather than the content of my little speech, conveyed better my disapproval of their activity. I then looked at my watch, pretended to be surprised at the lateness of the hour, and promptly dug both spurs into the mule's flanks, hoping to God that a bullet in the back of the head would not be forthcoming. The *baquiano* and I cantered on in silence to the chapel of Campana village.

Two or three hundred villagers kept me busy that evening. All the prayers were for peace in Nicaragua, and for the young men who were fighting — in both armies. While I heard individual confessions (confessions in wartime are particularly painful, and I find the experience more harrowing than any other of my duties as a priest) the people prayed the rosary for an end to the war. It was about 11 pm when the last penitent left and I strolled to the back of the chapel and was surprised to see three young contra soldiers gazing rather wistfully from outside the door, as if they felt impure or ineligible to set food inside.

During the week of June the priests and sisters of the Atlantic Coast attended the annual Study Week in Managua. Our theme this year (selected by ourselves to the slight chagrin of our two bishops) was 'The Spirituality of Liberation Theology', and we were directed by a Jesuit theologian from Guatemala. When I returned to Muelle de los Bueyes I was surprised to notice that all the chicks and pullets belonging to our neighbours had been painted with either green or pink! Apparently they had been getting confused, lost or stolen, so their owners had decided on a form of instant recognition. Anyway, the rainy season got underway a few days later and all the paint has been washed off.

After my first encounter with the contras I too feel as if some of my paint has come off in the wash.

Affectionately,

Padre Juan Luis (John Medcalf)

Parroquia Catolica
Muelle de los Bueyes
(''Ox-ford'')
Zelaya Central
Nicaragua
18 July 1987

Dear Friends,

Ox-ford (Zelaya Central) is beginning to look like Waterloo shortly before the battle, or the backstage of Edinburgh Castle during the Royal Tattoo. There are soldiers everywhere.

There is a regular (or professional) army unit living in tents overlooking the ford. These men impress me as well-disciplined and highly-motivated. A week ago I bumped into a group of off-duty regulars eating a boiled chicken (of third-world dimensions) and drinking a bottle of local rum. I was invited to join the treat, and for an hour or so I listened to their high-spirited accounts of how closely they'd come to being killed, but how they usually got the better of the cowardly contras.

Then there are the National Servicemen, aged between 17 and 25. Like NS men the world over (my own memories are vivid) they count the Days Done until the first year is completed, and then start counting the Days To Do as they begin their final year. Their typical greeting in the street, instead of *Buenos Días,* might be 'Only 269 to go!' A lot of them, I'm afraid, won't reach zero day. Church attendance is voluntary and several of them play guitars and drums to accompany the hymn singing.

A special company of uniformed vigilantes do a 4-month stint encamped around our river-bridges. Most of these are teachers and factory workers from the capital. We lend them books to read, since their only job is to guard the bridges against contra attack, though I must admit that one of these soldiers had us worried recently: He devoured *One Hundred Years of Solitude* in three days and then wanted to immerse himself in *War and Peace.* We had visions of bridges blowing up all round us while the novel-reading sergeant read on.

Finally there is what can only be called 'Dad's army,' a sort of Civil Defence for obese shopkeepers and travelling salesmen pushing forty. The fun-starved children of Ox-ford enjoy their half-hearted parades, and anxious wives contrive to slip them the odd *tortilla* when they march through Main Street.

The day after the chicken-and-rum fiesta I saw for the first time, a magnificent king vulture, white-tipped-with-black, its head and neck of brilliant orange and purplish blue. It was gorging itself on unidentifiable carrion, having driven off about 50 turkey buzzards, the common black vultures that scavenge in flocks. The following day Presidential Daniel Ortega announced that an average of 20 Nicaraguans are being killed every day in the US-financed war of aggression, and I dwelt on the morbid thought that vultures are the only creatures in this country not suffering from a chronic shortage of food.

Raw material for morbid thoughts has not been lacking. Hardly a day passes without an ambush, a skirmish or exploding mines. On July 3, a Franciscan brother, Tomás Zavaleta (40), was killed when his jeep was blown up by an anti-tank mine near Matagalpa. The parish priest, Fr. Ignacio (31), was gravely injured in the same explosion. Twelve of our parishioners from Jacinto Baca were mown down and killed by contra machine-gunners a week ago. News reached us yesterday of eight soldiers killed in an ambush nearby. On the same day we heard on the radio that President Reagan is going to ask Congress for another $130 million to continue this horrific bloodshed. Sister Helen (a nun from Wisconsin) was listening with me to the grim news when she uncharacteristically exploded with the words:

'I wish some guy would shoot *dead* that terrible Reagan!'

A lot of us here would echo Helen's death-wish, but I lay awake last night wondering randomly whether we don't transfer the guilt too easily. How many more Ethiopias and Nicaraguas are needed before people in wealthy countries stop voting for politicians who only promise to maintain or raise the living-standards of their electorate? Why can't they *see* that supermarkets stuffed with 35 different brands of chocolate bars and 22 assorted breakfast cereals are the *reason* why most people in most countries don't know what a chocolate bar is, and don't eat a breakfast at all?

I don't lose sleep easily, but I think it's not a bad idea for all of us to do so occasionally, if only to question some of our assumptions, and to strengthen the motivations of our lives — whether political, religious, humanitarian or to strengthen whatever else inspires us to work for fair play and justice in a world where vultures seem to rule the roost.

Affectionately,

Padre Juan Luis
(John Medcalf)

A DEATH IN NICARAGUA

This letter from Father Medcalf originally appeared in the British Catholic weekly newspaper, *The Tablet*.

A Franciscan friar was blown to eternity by an anti-tank mine in Nicaragua on 3 July. Not a very exceptional occurrence by contemporary Central American standards. After all, over 400 priests, friars and nuns (including one archbishop) have met with violent deaths in the present decade of turmoil and revolution in the half-dozen republics that form the narrow undernourished waistline of the New World. But there is something about this latest killing that may make it the most memorable and significant death since that of Archbishop Oscar Romero on 24 March 1980.

Thomas Zavaleta was born in El Salvador 40 years ago. His youthful idols were Francis of Assisi and the Beatles. He was the only friar in his graduation year to refuse priestly ordination, following the example of Francis himself. Thomas is remembered as an enthusiastic bottle-washer, whose energy for menial tasks was an example of the true Franciscan spirit. In the religious formation houses of Central America he became a well-known and much-loved brother to the novices and postulants of the Order of Friars Minor. There followed a six-year period in Rome, when he was chauffeur and batman for the Franciscan General.

His next appointment — to California — produced the only crisis of conscience he is known to have suffered. His superiors sensibly relented, and allowed him to forego the luxuries of life in the United States for the via dolorosa of his beloved Central America. His martyred fellow-countryman Oscar Romero would surely have approved the choice.

And so Brother Thomas was appointed, in April of this year, to the parish of Matiguas, in the central highlands of Nicaragua. His principal parish duty was to advise and help the cooperative of peasant farmers which had been set up by the parish priest two years previously, and which had become, with a membership of more than 1,000 families, the largest cooperative of its kind in the country. Brother Thomas must have known that these organisations are a prime target for Contra terrorism and that his option for the previously landless *campesinos* could invite reprisal.

In the late afternoon of 3 July relatives were concerned for the safety of two secretaries of the cooperative, Digna and Emperatriz. Thomas offered to drive the parish pick-up truck along the highway in search of the missing women. Fr. Ignacio Urbina, the parish priest, went with him. They discovered the two in a state of near-collapse at a distance of about 20 miles from the town of Matiguas. It was while they were returning home, in the fast-fading light, that the vehicle was blasted to smithereens by a mine buried in the unpaved potholed road. Thomas died at once, having received the fullest impact of the blast. Emperatriz failed to pull out of a coma and died the following day. Fr. Ignacio and Digna were later strapped to a pair of mules and taken to the nearest hospital; both are battling for survival as I write.

The third of July, according to the revised Roman calendar, is the official feast-day of St. Thomas the Apostle. The impetuous generosity of "Doubting Thomas" is recorded in the gospel of John, when Christ announces his intention of returning to Judea in spite of the risks, and Thomas says to his fellow disciples, "Let us also go, that we may die with him" (11:16).

The death of Thomas Zavaleta received front-page coverage here in Nicaragua. This may have been because this is virtually the only Central American republic where religious leaders have *not* been assassinated in the present decade. Only a few days before, President Daniel Ortega had announced that an average of 20 Nicaraguans are being killed each day in the war that is the horrific backcloth to our lives.

The official Sandinista daily, *Barricada,* affirmed that Zavaleta's death had been "planned" by the US-financed Contra rebels who were known to be present in the zone of Matiguas. The left-of-centre daily, *El Nuevo Diario,* agreed that the anti-tank mine had been planted by the Contras but demurred at the likelihood of a deliberate singling-out of the parish vehicle. At the other extreme, Radio Martí (the strident voice of Miami Cubans) accused the Sandinista Government of deliberately killing Zavaleta in order to discredit the Contras.

On Sunday 5 July Cardinal Miguel Obando y Bravo celebrated his customary morning Mass in the suburban church of Santo Domingo de las Sierritas. Perhaps he was still smarting under the accusation made two weeks previously by the

American magazine *Newsweek* that he had been a direct beneficiary of CIA funding. The small church was packed with journalists as the cardinal offered his condolences to the Franciscan Order and then proceeded to ask, "Who are guilty of his death?" This question, the cardinal said, "is asked in a very confused world where information is manipulated. Who were they? Only God knows". These somewhat inarticulate remarks from the Archbishop of Managua were interpreted by the Government as a challenge to their version of the death of Friar Thomas. For a short while it even looked as if the cardinal might be bundled on to a plane bound for Washington.

The crisis was defused on Monday 6 July when Fr. Damien Muratori, the Italian-born provincial superior of the Friars Minor of Central America, took a hand. He dispatched hundreds of telegrams (a cheap and efficient means of communication in Nicaragua) to religious communities throughout the country inviting them to attend "a reflection, Eucharist and *convivio*" on Friday 10 July in the Franciscan College of Managua "to celebrate the martyrdom of Friar Thomas". The event was attended by some two or three hundred priests, brothers and nuns. More important than counting heads, however, was the wide spectrum represented by the participants. Unfortunately, none of the 10 bishops made an appearance. The celebration was introduced by Fr. César Jerez, the Jesuit rector of the Catholic University. He was emphatic in his declaration that "Brother Thomas has been killed by a US-manufactured weapon in a US-financed war of aggression against Nicaragua". His fellow Jesuits were there in strength, as were the Dominicans — Sandinista supporters to a man. Present also were members of the powerful Salesian Order, to which Cardinal Obando belongs, known for their opposition to the Sandinista government. Fr. Miguel D'Escoto, the Maryknoll priest-cum-Foreign Minister, kept a discreetly low profile at the back of the church. The centre of the stage, however, was held on this particular evening by the followers of St. Francis. In an impassioned sermon, Fr. Damian Muratori declared that "the Catholic Church in Central America is very deeply divided. The death of Friar Thomas must serve to lessen that division so that we can be more effective as leaven in the mass".

We formed small groups to discuss the question, "What practical steps can we take to hasten the coming of peace in our land?" The enthusiasm generated by the richness of the replies was contagious: "We urge our bishops to renew their dialogue with the Government'' (broken off several months ago); ''Let us have round-the-clock prayer vigils at the bedsides of the war victims''; ''Let us give up calling each other 'revolutionaries' and 'anti-revolutionaries''' (easier said than done). The two proposals most heartily accepted were that the Franciscan family should continue to take the initiative in bringing unity and peace to the Church and the nation, and that a special ceremony should be held in Matiguas at the beginning of August to mark the traditional ''month's mind'' for Friar Thomas, when it is hoped that the local bishop will preside or at least be present. These proposals were accepted unanimously. Perhaps their implementation will mark a step forward in the process of reconciliation.

Meanwhile, in neighbouring El Salvador, you can still see car-stickers that read: *Haga Patria: Mate A Un Cura* (Be Patriotic: Kill a Priest).

Parroquia
Muelle de los Bueyes
("Ox-ford")
Zelaya Central
Nicaragua

16 August 1987

Dear Friends,

There is a rustle of peace in the Nicaraguan air. The dove seems to have challenged the vulture. Ever since the five Central American presidents signed the historic peace agreement in Guatemala City on August 7 there has been an uncanny atmosphere here in Central Zelaya, like that of war-weary soldiers readying themselves at long last to lift their heads out of the trenches.

I deserted my own trench a few weeks ago to attend the International Book Fair in Managua. After all, we are partly in the book business ourselves, trying to prevent the return of illiteracy by providing books and magazines of use and interest to our peasant farmers in the Ox-ford parish and beyond. The Fair had been the brainchild of Ernesto Cardenal (poet, priest, Minister of Culture) and of the director of the Frankfurt Book Fair, the world's largest. I arrived for the inauguration ceremony and was surprised to see the President and half the Cabinet in attendance. I had forgotten that praying and poetry-writing come easier to most of them than politicking and demagoguery.

The US stand was the most eye catching, dominated, it seemed, by lavishly illustrated biographies of Nancy Reagan and the publications of Gay Books Incorporated — no censorship here. The Soviet booth was unsensational by comparison — Gorbachev's speeches in a ballbearing factory, redeemed by an exquisite series of children's books. The British were represented by two religious publishers, Burns & Oates and Sheed & Ward, and by Zed Books (an independent left-wingish house). I looked in vain for 'Winnie El Pooh' in Spanish translation.

I returned to Ox-ford in the open back of a timber lorry, a fresh and exhilarating experience (I counted eleven different species of butterflies in an hour) until a tropical storm turned me and the other fifty-odd hitchhikers into a sodden mass of miserable humanity. The sun came out again very suddenly, and caused us all to steam like puddings in a pressure cooker. Nicaragua, say the brochures, is a land of contrasts.

The following day I visited Monkey Face village. Amanda, the midwife/catechist, took me to see the latest refugee family, a woman and her five children who had fled from their mountain home when the husband had been kidnapped by the contras a few weeks before. I also tried to comfort 22-year old Pedrito, a professional soldier in the Sandinista army who had just received news that a platoon of contras had kidnapped, and probably killed, two more members of his family: his aunt and his young male cousin. Pedrito's wife, Elsa, helps us out in the kitchen occasionally, but her congenital asthma reaches the limits of tolerance at moments of great stress. These are the war casualties that statistics don't cover.

On August 7, Muelle de los Bueyes was attacked at 3:15 in the morning. For nearly an hour, battle raged between the attacking contras and the Sandinista regular army unit that defends this village. The din of machine-guns and the red lights of the mortars were infernal, but this time there was no screaming by civilians, as in the previous attack in April. We are losing our innocence. The attack took place in the aptly-named Death Canyon, at 1 kilometer from the church and shops.

When dawn came, soon after 5 o'clock, I crossed the road to the convent and discovered that a bullet had pierced the timber bedroom used by Sister Helen, only a foot or so above her pillow. Fortunately she, like most of the population, had dashed to a dugout when the battle began. A 12-year old boy, who had not left his bed, had been wounded by flying shrapnel and was later taken to hospital by Fr. Bernard Boulang, a priest from Normandy assigned to work with me in this parish. A few roofs were badly damaged, church windows shattered, and a chattering, nervous village could hardly believe that nobody had died in the moonlight, unless the armies had already buried their dead.

The same evening of Friday, 7 August, we heard on our radios the long-awaited and scarcely-believable news: The five Central American presidents had signed a peace agreement that could bring a ceasefire within 90 days. As I write this letter we have known almost ten days without fighting, ten hope-filled days that are like the scent of jasmine after a tropical storm. I must run over the road to post this letter quickly before something happens to take away this hope.

Affectionately,

Padre Juan Luis Medcalf

Parroquia Catolica
Muelle de los Bueyes
("Ox-ford")
Zelaya Central
Nicaragua
20 September 1987

Dear Friends,

A few months ago a priest colleague in New York sent me a book entitled *Preservation of Personal Health in Warm Climates.* One night last week I lay in bed with my mosquito bed-net tucked in on all sides, with nothing better to read. I was horrified to learn of all the fatal bites, diseases and fevers rampant in the tropics, most of which I seemed to have missed by the skin of my teeth in the last 20 years. Especially repellent was a photograph of an adult mosquito magnified 35 times. I began to feel as if malaria was creeping up my body from my toes. Only a neat double rum brought on sleep.

It seems as if the atmosphere in Nicaragua over the past few weeks has been full of malaria, blowing hot one day, blowing cold the next. Since the signing of the Central American peace agreement of August 7, we have all been caught up in a race against time to bring an end to the war.

Our hopes rose high when Cardinal Obando y Bravo accepted the presidency of a National Commission of Peace and Reconciliation. But the following day Mr. Reagan made a special broadcast on a clandestine radio station in which he promised to keep money flowing to the contras.

Then temperatures went up again at a mass meeting in Juigalpa City, attended by political and religious leaders of all shades, when it seemed that everybody was willing to make the Peace Agreement work.

A few nights later, we were saddened when a few Sandinista soldiers got very drunk here in Muelle and started firing machine-guns into the air. One soldier was badly wounded, but no civilians were hurt. I suppose the soldiers are under even greater stress than we are, and the rum is cheap.

At local levels also Peace Commissions have been formed. Our Sister Agnes Fischer is a member, and she may soon be travelling to neighbouring Costa Rica to speak with the young men who fled there to avoid army conscription. From our parish alone, there must be two or three thousand men living in refugee camps just over the border. They, too, will benefit from a cease-fire.

But then we had the chilling news a week ago that President

Reagan is torpedoing all these efforts by demanding $270 million from Congress for more contra aid!

Meanwhile our parish youth club (all-female since the males are fighting or in hiding) marched 40 kilometers along the highway, singing songs and hymns for peace. In Washbasin Village *(La Batea),* a huge peace banner hangs over the door of the chapel, and the villagers are trying to revive the ancient right of sanctuary, inviting the contras to lay down their arms and seek refuge in the chapel. Many of our more isolated villages want to follow this example.

On September 7, I visited the regional prison, near Juigalpa. There were roughly 500 prisoners-of-war (or political prisoners, according to which side you support) several of whom were parishioners from Muelle. The physical conditions of the prison were excellent, and the prisoners have many opportunities for education and sport. Their chief complaint was against small food rations, but that is a common complaint outside the prison as well. I was reminded of the late Cardinal Heenan's custom when visiting foreign countries — he would spurn official banquets and insist on going to a jail and a hospital, declaring that a country could be best judged by the way it treated its prisoners and its sick.

Throughout the country most parishes — Catholic and Evangelical — seem to be suspending many of their normal activities in order to promote a ceasefire by November 7, the agreed deadline. The date seems frighteningly near, and there is a lot to be done.

In the last month, three Catholic priests have been jailed in the US for opposing their government's war-mongering in Central America, and Vietnam war veteran Brian Wilson had his legs amputated by a train carrying arms for the contras. The forces of evil seem very strong when seen from a small under-nourished banana republic trying to defend its dignity.

I learned the other day that the contra chief I met in June is known as The Bull *(El Toro).* There is another of higher rank with the pseudonym The Devil *(El Diablo),* also in this area. In mid-October, I hope to meet up with the second of these during one of my bush trips. Perhaps I can persuade him or some of his men to lay down their arms. Or perhaps I am being naive. Whatever happens I should be able to write an interesting appendix to the book I mentioned at the beginning of this letter. God bless the Devil!

Affectionately,

P. Juan Luis
(John Medcalf)

Parroquia Catolica
Muelle de los Bueyes
("Ox-ford")
Zelaya Central
Nicaragua

19 October 1987

Dear Friends,

The last few days have been the worst in my life so far. On October 15, this village of Muelle was attacked by over 500 well-equipped contras. The battle began at 3 a.m. and continued uninterrupted until 6 a.m. The din of mortars, machine-guns and ricocheting shrapnel was horrendous. The attackers penetrated simultaneously at three different points — the highroad, the bridge over Monkey River, and Death Canyon. Their chief objective was probably to blow up the bridge.

The contras surged into several of the village streets. We heard them shouting slogans ('You can *keep* your amnesty!' etc). The Sandinistas made a temporary retreat, only to return with reinforcements for the street fighting. The bridge was saved, and the contras dispersed when their supply of ammunition came to an end.

We opened up the parish hall to the wounded and dead. They were brought in from all parts of the village. Our canvas stretcher-beds were quickly drenched in blood since we used them for those worst wounded. Others were laid on the tiled floor. I have so many indelible impressions of that day — cutting a soldier's clothes off his body with scissors as he screamed with pain; a young man seizing my hand with an iron grip as he groaned 'I'm dying. I can't bear the pain!'; a baby girl of about 20 months just staring ahead as the blood soaked her clothes; the terrible vacant look caused by shell shock on the faces of teenage soldiers; the stench of human excrement, urine and blood before the nuns and nurses were able to clean up the patients. There were more than 30 gravely injured and 20 dead. The morning seemed endless as we waited for an ambulance to transport the most urgent cases to the hospital.

Rumours began to reach us that four other towns and villages had been attacked that night, including La Batea just seven kilometers west of Muelle. At 2 pm a Sandinista driver made a bad mistake. Having found the dead bodies of three contras near the bridge, he strung them up on the back of his open lorry, heads down, like sides of beef bound for an unhygienic market. The driver's fury was understandable, but many villagers protested as he drove through the streets with the almost naked bodies waving grotesquely. I spoke with the mayor and we agreed to give them christian burial in a common grave in the village cemetery, as soon as possible. There were no more coffins available by this hour of the day, but by 4 pm the three soldiers had been buried in plastic sheeting, and a rustic cross marks their grave.

So much for the Central American Peace Agreement! Just a few days before the attack I had visited the next-door republic of Costa Rica with Sisters Helen and Agnes. I heard President Oscar Arias speak to university students about the Peace Plan that bears his name, and that won him this year's Nobel Peace Prize. There seemed to be so much enthusiasm and determination to make the plan work. But I should have been warned. Near the border with Nicaragua, on our way back, we stopped at the refugee camp at Tilarán, where nearly 3,000 Nicaraguans live in squalid conditions. When we attempted to speak with them we met with such hostility on the part of a few, and craven fear on the part of the others, that we gave up the effort and drove on. It was obvious that the contras had complete control within the barbed-wire fence.

I have not yet met the 'Devil' (mentioned in my last letter) and I probably never will now. However, I visited a village called Green Folds on September 28, and as I heard confessions at the back of the chapel the deacon interrupted me to say that two contra leaders were outside and wanted to talk. It was nearly 11 pm and a moonless night. For over an hour I listened to a diatribe against the Sandinista government and a warning not to let myself be 'manipulated' by atheistic hordes. The leaders then shook my hand and walked off into the jungle, followed by a platoon of about ten men. Once again I should have been warned.

My way home from Green Folds the next morning took me through some of the most beautiful jungle I have ever known. At one point I saw a cuddly bear-like animal a few feet above my head. It turned out to be a sloth, and it was curled round a branch and upside down. My guide said that sloths sleep 18 hours a day. Also for the first time I became aware of the wonder of orchids — so many designs and colours, most of them resting in the join between the trunk and the bough of a tree, but not as parasites as is commonly thought, simply being supported and receiving moisture. It must be pleasant to be an orchid or a sloth.

God bless us all, and especially these poor people of Nicaragua.

P. Juan Luis
(John Medcalf)

Parroquia Catolica
Muelle de los Bueyes
("Ox-ford")
Zelaya Central
Nicaragua
18 November 1987

Dear Friends,

A month ago it seemed impossible that Central Zelaya could ever be normal again. The savage attacks on civilian targets on the night of October 15 removed any doubts we had concerning the intentions of the contras. In Muelle alone over 30 died, many are maimed for life, and there are widows in every street. As we lined up for bread the other morning I heard one woman say to another, 'Lucky the mothers who have no sons!' But even this consolation is unfounded: two houses away from this parish church, the three young daughters of the man who sells rum and cigarettes were all wounded in the legs by shrapnel. One of them may never walk again. In comparison, the five-inch wide hole in my tin roof was nothing. I merely got a few drenchings before it was mended.

Digging underground shelters has been the most common domestic activity since the attack. The extreme dampness of the soil makes this a hazardous job, but pneumonia is a better bet than a bullet through the head, I suppose.

Then came November, and All Souls' Day. The shops were full of multicoloured wreaths of paper flowers waiting for buyers to place them on the graves in the over-crowded village cemetery. In one shop a wag was so moved by the beauty of this peasant handicraft that he called out in a loud voice: 'Roll on death, to get a wreath!'

Thank God for the humorists who keep us from indulgence in self-pity or self-importance. It's a shame the office of King's jester has died out. Some of our more intransigent world leaders might act with more compassion if they could really laugh at themselves occasionally, instead of merely dispensing plastic smiles to the media men.

On All Souls' Day we also had a visit from a Scottish bishop, Maurice Taylor of Galloway, and three other church leaders from Britain. Their words of encouragement to the people in two villages were greatly appreciated, and although they were kept awake by machine-gun fire, I was glad that none of them needed a floral wreath.

On November 8 the local army unit invited our church choir to the hill that overlooks the strategic bridge over Monkey

River. It was here that 25 soldiers had been killed in the defence of the bridge on October 15. We sang a mixed program of hymns and Sandinista songs in honour of the dead, and the presence of the teenage choirgirls in their simple cotton dresses was the perfect distraction for the young soldiers who were mourning their dead companions. I afterwards chatted with a soldier who had interrupted his seminary studies with the Jesuits in order to defend his country. I hope he becomes a bishop one day.

Last Friday, after visiting the village school, I noticed a small group of people huddled together in a way that suggested an accident. A young soldier lay stretched out in pain on the grass beside the road. He had had his right leg amputated as a result of the October 15 battle and had been trying out his home-made crutches for the first time when he fell. Several of us helped him back to the tiny hut where he lives with his parents and his wife. His name is José Angel. He was 18 last July, and has been a soldier for ten years! His father and his older brother had put on uniforms before him, so perhaps it was a case of not wanting to be the odd man out. But it was much more than that somehow. José's mother told me how she learned to read and write as a result of the Sandinista Literacy Campaign of 1980. She didn't need to tell me how that event had transformed her life and given her a new dignity within her family and village.

When the contras stepped up their activities, the entire family abandoned their cattle farm and came to live in Ox-ford as refugees. José Angel found himself a wife called Sabina, who is expecting their first child, due around Christmas. On the night of October 15 he was patrolling our churchyard when enemy troops overwhelmed the village. Several bullets penetrated his leg, face and arms. He lay helpless in a pool of blood until the battle was over.

Last Sunday we brought José Angel and his family to mass in the parish jeep. He sat proudly, still uniformed, between his wife and his mother in the church building he had helped save from destruction. I don't know what the future holds for him and for so many who are maimed for life as a result of this cruel, unjust war.

If every reader of this letter were to write to the US Ambassador, perhaps Christmas this year would be less trivial.

God bless,

John Medcalf
(Padre Juan Luis)

Parroquia Catolica
Muelle de los Bueyes
("Ox-ford")
Zelaya Central
Nicaragua

23 December 1987

Dear Friends,

Good news has been scarce this month, but there has been some. José Angel, the teenage soldier who lost a leg when the contras attacked Muelle on October 15, became a first-time father on November 22 to a healthy son, also to be called José. His father was in a Managua hospital, being prepared for an artificial leg, when José junior was being born in their square timber hut (each wall about twelve feet long) with a palm frond roof.

On December 2, we remembered Zacarías Garzón, beloved church-worker from Turkey Hens village who was savagely tortured and killed by the contras just a year before. Somebody had heard that I play the violin (badly), and I was handed the instrument that Zacarías had carved and that he used to play to accompany the hymn-singing. I felt strangely moved when picking it up and am still not sure whether the villagers mean me to keep it.

The following day Señora Alicia, our next-door neighbour, made a delicious stew with a reddish squirrel that her small son had killed with a slingshot in the churchyard. This was a killing I could condone, so I shared in the spoils.

The day of the squirrel stew, we heard that one of the 20 or so priests of our diocese of Bluefields, Hector Molina (Nicaraguan and newly-ordained), has decided to enlist with the Sandinista Reservists to defend his parish town of Siuna. The nuns told me that Bishop Schlaefer is 'saddened' by his decision but is not taking any disciplinary action. I can understand Father Hector's impatience with the way things are going, though I think he has acted unwisely. But then, this is not my country, as it is his, and I can always salve my conscience by writing these circular letters. Perhaps his position is no more anomalous than that of so many uniformed army chaplains in the so-called Christian West.

I was glad to put aside these problems last week and go on a bush trip to the outlying villages and farmsteads of Central

Zelaya. I enjoy riding a horse or mule through the cattle ranches, and more especially through the remnants of jungle which sadly are being cut down at an alarming speed. There is plenty of wildlife to observe between villages. My one regret is that I have not yet seen the spectacular quetzal bird, found only in the heart of the rain forests. It is a very timid creature, distinguished by its very long green-and-red tail feathers and an upstanding downy crest, and all five Central American republics claim it as theirs and endow it with magical qualities. No quetzal has survived in captivity. Some ornithologists declare the quetzal to be the most beautiful of the world's birds. Anyway, I haven't yet seen one.

The first village in my bush trip was Avocado Pear. Things started well enough: A hundred or so farming families joined me in praying for an end to the drought, and the clouds burst within an hour. But the onset of the rain brought with it another problem: the contras. I noticed about ten of them ride up to the chapel as I was preaching on one of Isaiah's great Advent prophecies. They heard nought for their comfort, and I hoped they didn't sense the nervous pain in my stomach as I spoke about swords being turned into ploughshares in the context of Nicaragua and our hopes for peace.

I found sleep difficult that night in Avocado Pear. I tried to read by paraffin lamp one of those delightful medieval whodunits by Ellis Peters, against a background of civil war in 12th Century England, and the monk-detective Brother Cadfael tiptoeing through the herb gardens and graveyards of Shrewsbury.

Nicaragua, however, is not experiencing a civil war, but a naked aggression financed by Washington. Of this I am convinced.

As I continued my pastoral visiting to the other villages (Silence, The Bell, The Angels, Christ the King and Iguana), this impression was strengthened. Of course there are faults on the other side. I spent two and half hours investigating a rocket fired by the Sandinistas from a distance of twelve miles which had shattered rocks and trees. There were isolated stories of forced recruitment into the Sandinista army. In Christ the King village, I had to ask a patrol of 20 soldiers to move on, so as not to invite an attack by the contras while the chapel was filled with civilians.

It was while the choir was rehearsing Christmas Carols in Iguana Village that I heard on the BBC Overseas Service that the Zelaya mining towns of Bonanza, Rosita and Siuna had been attacked by 7000 contras. Fr. Hector Molina is parish priest of Siuna. Now, 48 hours later, we are still waiting for official numbers of dead and wounded. And the names.

Peace in Central America is as elusive as the quetzal.

God bless you,

Padre Juan Luis
(John Medcalf)

1988

Parroquia Cristo Redentor
Muelle de los Bueyes
("Ox-ford")
Zelaya Central
Nicaragua

24 January 1988

Dear Friends,

There was no truce in Nicaragua for Christmas. The war carried on as usual, and people were killed as they have been for the last seven years. This did not prevent a lot of peasant farmers and their families getting together to eat chicken and sing carols. In Washtub Village we had a boisterous Midnight Mass, sobered only by the reading aloud of the long list of war dead and the supplications for peace.

On Christmas Day afternoon, several of us drove 30 miles to La Esperanza (Hope Town!) for an inter-parish party. We had a couple of hours of relaxation before having to attend to two lorries full of refugee families who were coming in to sleep at the parish centre for fear of a rumoured attack by the contras.

A few days later, Muelle de los Bueyes buzzed with traffic, mostly army jeeps and motorcycles. We all became anxious, especially when helicopters flew over Main Street. Rumors circulated. The truth was a welcome relief: President Daniel Ortega was coming to our village on New Year's Eve to deliver his message to the nation.

Considering our position in the middle of the war zone, the preparations for Ortega's visit were surprisingly lax. Mariachi bands played in the streets in the early morning, and we were encouraged by loudspeakers to walk two kilometers to meet the President. About 700 of the 2000 villagers accepted the invitation. We waited on the battlefield where 25 Sandinista soldiers had been killed on October 15, and at 9:30 am the President arrived in an army jeep, wearing his usual olive-green battledress. I was chatting with the survivors of the battle when he arrived, and there was a momentary lull of incomprehension when a captain presented us all as 'the survivors of Pancasán Company.' The President laughed aloud when I hastily explained that although indeed a survivor I was not of the Pancasán

Company, but the Catholic parish priest of the area. Speeches followed. The President announced for the first time the motto for the coming year, 1988 — 'Peace with Dignity: A Free Fatherland or Death.' Television cameras recorded the event (it was fun to see ourselves later that day on the TV screen) and there were kisses and embraces for everybody in typical Latin American fashion. Even our parish nuns (from Wisconsin) treasured their presidential hugs.

Meanwhile, back in the village, a dozen women had been cooking four cows so that everybody could have a good lunch. The children were all given a sturdy inflatable toy (made in the Soviet Union, but the children weren't worried about that, nor was I: no other country had thought of sending Christmas toys to the children of Nicaragua's war zone.). The final gift for Ox-ford was a real telephone, so that we can dial to any part of the world. Unfortunately, the following day the contras blew up certain installations, so that only three overseas calls could be made before we sank back into isolation once more.

On January 2, I wrote in my new diary that 'an extraordinary loud thunderclap with a very bright lightning flash caused me to jump off my bed in sheer panic.'

By January 3, I had written that 'it was not thunder last night but an anti-aircraft missile that fell at the bottom of the garden.'

Two days later we had a diocesan assembly here in Muelle. 60 priests, sisters and deacons from Central and South Zelaya met for a four-day policy-making session. The emphasis was on the efforts for peace in Central America, and what we were doing or failing to do in our respective parishes. Our two US-born bishops came in for a lot of criticism. Most of us could not understand why the 300 Catholic bishops in the USA had condemned (in November) Reagan's support for the contra rebels while our men on the spot kept silent. The most charitable and the most generalized interpretation was that they are frightened, or, perhaps more accurately, have been frightened. In any case, the assembly unanimously signed a circular letter supporting the Arias Peace Plan and condemning by implication the notorious interference by the US in Nicaraguan affairs.

We now have three national daily newspapers (not bad for a population of only three millions) representing the entire spectrum of political opinion. I was surprised, on January 15, to notice that all three had a very similar front-page headline —

'USA Puts Pressure on Central American Presidents.' The occasion was the summit meeting in Costa Rica when the five presidents tried desperately hard to salvage the Peace Plan.
I still haven't seen that elusive quetzal.

Affectionately,
Padre Juan Medcalf

Parish of Christ Redeemer
Muelle de los Bueyes
Zelaya Central
Nicaragua
2 February 1988

Dear Bishops Salvador and Paul:

This is a farewell to you both, my shepherds in Christ, at the end of 20 years of missionary work in Latin America, the last 2½ of which I have spent as pastor here in Muelle de los Bueyes. I am not leaving Nicaragua in a mood of frustration, but because I feel I can do more for peace from my native England, and the present tragedy demands that each one of us should do what he can where he feels he can be most effective.

I am aware that you, Bishop Paul, dislike letters as a form of communication. At the last annual Assembly of the Bluefields Vicariate you warned us that letters "are open to bad interpretations". Nevertheless, during the same assembly, you showed wisdom in accepting the unanimous desire of 60 priests, nuns and other pastoral agents, allowing a circular letter to be drawn up and read publicly in all the churches and chapels of our vicariate. This document approved unreservedly the "Arias Plan" and by implication condemned the notorious interference of the Reagan Administration. The Letters of your namesake the Apostle Paul have also been "open to bad interpretation" as well as a cause of division over the 2000 years of christianity, but we do not for these reasons regard them as dangerous reading.

I return to my country of origin deeply impressed by the moral strength of the Nicaraguan people, especially by the suffering of the farm workers of Zelaya. I am equally fortified by the example of most of the priests, nuns and deacons — both Nicaraguan and foreign — with whom it has been my privilege to work. As for yourselves, the two US-born Capuchin bishops of Zelaya, I expressed my admiration for the pluralism you have allowed and you continue to allow. Zelaya is perhaps the only part of Nicaragua where priests and nuns are not persecuted and expelled by their bishops for their political convictions. To say this is to say a lot. The anti-evangelical intolerance of the majority of the native bishops does not exist on the Atlantic Coast, thanks be to God.

At the same time I feel obliged to tell you that mere tolerance or silence is not sufficient in the terrible circumstances of the present war. I would have liked to have heard the clear and decisive voice of my bishops on several occasions whilst I was pastor of Muelle de los Bueyes parish. Here are two instances among many I would quote.

On October 15 this town was the target of an attack that resulted in more than 30 deaths, both military and civilian. Within a few weeks I received dozens of letters and telegrams of condolence and solidarity from Europe and other parts . . . but from yourselves there was not a word of consolation for the mourners, nor a breath of condemnation for those responsible for this crime.

A month after the attack over 300 US bishops (with only one abstention) condemned Reagan's support for the "contras" as "legally dubious and morally wrong". An excellent opportunity was presented to the two US bishops working in Nicaragua, eye-witnesses of so many crimes committed by the government of their country of origin, to show solidarity with their brother bishops in the USA. But once again the silence was deathly and shameful.

In spite of your allergy to letters and public declarations I believe — with the author of the book of Ecclesiastes — that there is "a time for silence, and a time to speak out", a time to write and a time to abstain from writing.

> *"I tell you, if these (disciples of Jesus) are silent the very stones would cry out" (Luke 19, 40).*

May our discrepancies not impede our brotherhood in Christ.

God bless you,

John Medcalf

This letter was published in Spanish in two of Nicaragua's three daily newspapers ("Barricada" and "El Nuevo Diario") a few days after being sent to the two bishops.

7 Temple Court
Temple Road
Canterbury
Kent

10 April 1988

Dear Friends,

This is a sort of epilogue to the 25 letters I have written from my Nicaraguan parish since November 1985. My final days in Ox-ford were tense because of the frequent black-outs and the noise of nearby combat. On my last Sunday I acted out, with the help of young people, the story of Jonah and the Whale. This ridiculous but inspired tale has always seemed to me to have a lot to say about human folly and divine love and is Jewish humour at its best. In Managua, on the day I left, about 25 *gringos* were fasting outside the US Embassy, convinced that their fast could stop the war. Just like Jonah the Sandwich-Board Man in Niniveh City.

I had long since promised myself a fairly leisurely trip back to England, travelling mostly by bus through the other Central American republics. I also wished to compare notes with colleagues working in similar conditions. My first country was El Salvador, a place that horrified me from the moment of arrival. I simply cannot write the names of the many brave people I met. Their lives would be in immediate danger. However, it *is* safe for me to say that while six native Franciscans were making their solemn vows of poverty, chastity and obedience in a large and crowded church, we were 'buzzed' by low-flying military helicopters throughout the ceremony. I can also report that Bishop Rosa Chávez at his customary 8 am Sunday mass in San Salvador Cathedral, denounced the Salvadoran police forces for killing 26 men, women and children in the previous week. He read out the names of the dead to a hushed congregation, and the Monday morning newspapers called him a 'communist stooge.' Like Jonah's whale, I wanted to vomit.

A plane took me over guerilla-held territory to Tegucigalpa, capital of Honduras. At the airport I was detained for an hour and subjected to stupid interrogation ('Are you a revolutionary?' 'Which side do you think will win the war?' etc.), presumably because of the Nicaraguan permit in my passport. There are about 5000 US troops stationed in Honduras, and I had the amazingly good fortune to visit two top-security US army camps, where I found it convenient to mislay my tell-tale passport. I tried my best to disturb the consciences of five American chaplains, four of whom carried the rank (and salary!) of colonel. It was in Honduras that I saw what I had never seen in Nicaragua — the pot-bellies of starving children. The Spanish word 'honduras' means 'the depths.' A modern American translation would be 'the pits,' a fairly apt name for the poorest country in the New World after Haiti.

I was driven to the Guatemalan border by American Franciscans who were deeply ashamed of their government's performance in Central America. They were a welcome relief after the colonel-chaplains. A short bus-ride took me to the popular religious shrine of Esquipulas, where an unhurried and uninterrupted line of Indians file past a 'black Christ' above the high altar, kissing and stroking the wood. It was in this shimmering white abbey church that a peace agreement was signed by five Central American presidents in August 1987.

Guatemala is a beautiful country of lakes and volcanos, but nearly everything and everybody has been debased by a long succession of viciously violent governments. Even the currency has been named after the elusive bird of the rain forests, the quetzal, so that a newspaper costs half a quetzal and a rum-and-coke costs two quetzals.

Close to the abbey, an Indian woman of 35 spoke to me for over an hour of the terrible night six years ago when the convent where she was employed as cook was attacked by 15 policemen at 2 am. They dragged away Sister Victoria, who had recently returned from a visit to Nicaragua and had dared to speak favourably of the Sandinista Revolution to a group of youths in Esquipulas. One of the policemen later blew the whistle, but Victoria's tortured raped body has never been discovered.

On February 21 I crossed into southern Mexico, where I followed the route of *The Power and The Glory* and *The Lawless Roads* taken by Graham Greene exactly 50 years before. The ex-British colony of Belize was my final Central American country, after which a huge whale swallowed me whole and disgorged me in Heathrow Airport on March 27.

I wish to thank the many persons responsible for distributing and publishing these letters, particularly Robert Copsey and my sister Kathy Doust. It seems that several thousand people have received photo-copies, and several newspapers and magazines regularly published the letters in full or part. The parish Ox-ford is enjoying a precarious but hopeful cease-fire, and the Rural Library program is being handed over to

Nicaraguan leaders by Paddy Welsh. My own immediate future includes speaking and writing engagements and any other activities that can make better known the plight of the Latin American people whose lives I have shared for most of my 25 years as a Catholic priest. This is for me, I hope, the sign of Jonah.

Affectionately,
John Medcalf

8 July 1988

Dear Friends in Nicaragua,

I promised to send you my impressions of Britain, so here's my first "reverse letter". After all, I wrote 25 letters to British friends from my parish of Muelle de los Bueyes so perhaps you will enjoy learning something about the country that used to send pirates and African slaves to your Caribbean coast.

In fact I am writing this from Bristol, a large English port whose wealth came chiefly from slave-trading; there are two elegant cathedrals and lots of smaller churches, but I doubt whether the congregations think much about the slaves.

It is midsummer here, and not a vulture or a quetzal in sight. There are thousands of US troops, however, but nobody talks about them, perhaps because they keep a lower profile than in Central America. I am touring the country talking about Nicaragua — in parishes, schools, universities, seminaries and trade union meeting-halls. Anywhere with a congregation or an audience.

I get a bit depressed sometimes with some of my brother priests: so many of them are caught up in administrative tasks that the laity could do better; so many don't seem to notice that young people are almost totally absent from their churches. Fortunately a lot of towns have a university chaplaincy, where the young-at-heart Christians can find an oasis — or, perhaps, just a clearing in the rain-forest.

The Catholic bishops here don't normally have any kind of Pastoral Plan for their dioceses, which will strike you as strange; they are also hypersensitive about politics, and don't give much of a lead in matters like Northern Ireland and nuclear war.

You may be amused to hear that this month the great Peruvian theologian Gustavo Gutierrez is to address the Lambeth Conference of the Anglican Church. It is difficult to imagine the Catholic bishops inviting such a "wolf" into their sheepfold! The ironic thing, of course, is that in spite of all the recent debates about liberation theologies, the only continent that has produced a schism or heresy since Vatican II is Europe, with the Archbishop Lefebvre affair. So much for Europe being the bastion of orthodoxy!

British youths divide into two tribes: the yuppies and the yobbos. There is a lot of good in both groups, but people who belong to neither group pretend they are loathsome. Yuppies are well-heeled and grow better in the south. Yobbos are mostly northerners and are frequently unemployed.

Both groups give religion and politics a wide berth. A few weeks ago there was a well-organised BBC Pop Concert to celebrate Nelson Mandela's 70th birthday. Nearly 70 countries tuned in and umpteen millions were watching. So far so good. It was a golden opportunity for both British tribes to proclaim a message to the world.

Sadly, however, the only banner visible in the vast Wembley Stadium read "Hi Mum". The yuppification and the yobbification of Britain are plain to everybody, but neither the Church nor the politicians seem to care or notice.

Yes, I do miss the beans and rice, and the occasional fried iguana! Most of all I miss all of you — your warm faith and your determination to make the world a lovelier place, more full of love that is. At the same time, I am enjoying my native England and sharing my Nicaraguan experiences with a wide variety of people. There is a lot of good will, and there are a lot of small groups outside the big structures who need encouraging.

In a way I feel like one of those Bristol pirates who plied the ocean between our two continents centuries ago. The difference is that I didn't find any gold, though what I did find is far more valuable. Let us keep each other, and our countries, in our mutual thoughts and prayers.

John Medcalf

St. Peter's Church
Shoreham-by-Sea
West Sussex
Inglaterra

November 24, 1988

Dear Friends in Nicaragua,

I can hardly believe the horrific news of the devastation caused last month by Hurricane Joan. There has been almost nothing in the newspapers over here. I quoted some of your letters from the pulpit last Sunday and almost broke down with emotion as I read out "400,000 Nicaraguans homeless, 70 per cent of the rain forests destroyed". Why should it happen to you of all people?

But the parishioners here at St. Peter's were very generous. They raised nearly £1000 in a special collection, and this should provide quite a few corrugated metal roofs for your homes and schools.

Several of you made me laugh with a phrase you use in your letters. You ask whether I'm "settling down" or "settling in" here in Shoreham-by-Sea. That's just what the people here are continually asking me as well. How can I "settle" when I think of your homes and crops flattened by a hurricane? Only broody hens settle. What worries me is that sometimes I get the impression from fellow priests that by "settling down" they mean "getting on with the real job in a real part of the world", as if you all belonged to an exotic world of fantasy!

Anyway, I'm trying hard not to be a broody hen. The people in my new parish have made me feel very welcome, and are genuinely interested in everything that is happening to you and your Latin American homelands.

A few Sundays ago I suggested in my sermon that Ernesto "Che" Guevara could teach us Christians a thing or two about love, perseverance and dedication. I was accused of preaching terrorism by only one person out of the 500 strong congregation, and he is a retired banker.

A headteacher made the interesting point that "Che" Guevara's wife was worthy of canonisation for allowing her husband to gallivant around Cuba and Bolivia while she looked after their five children. I thought afterwards that there are passages in the Gospel that are meant for laypeople as well as priests in time of crisis: "Unless a man leaves his wife, his children, his lands for my sake . . . he cannot be my disciple."

The important thing is that a lot of the people over here do respond to a challenge and aren't content just to drift along like dead dogs in a stream. In spite of everything — Hurricane Joan, the debt crisis, the US Election results (Apathy No. 1, Bush No. 2, Dukakis No. 3) — I share your faith and optimism that we can create a better world, and that Christian communities are vitally important to inject joy and love into the new creation.

My bishop rang me up last night. You can guess his opening question: "Are you settling in alright, John?"

Very affectionately,
Padre Juan Luis

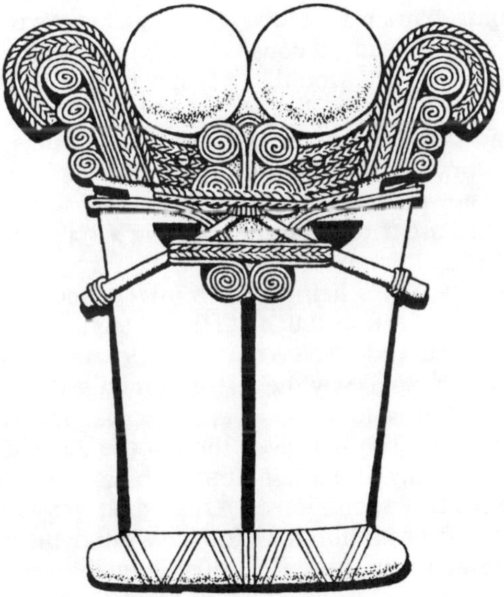

St. Peter's Church
Shoreham-by-Sea
West Sussex
Inglaterra

9 December 1988

Dear Friends in Latin America

I have a sneaking suspicion that some of my parishioners are smugglers. After all, Shoreham-by-Sea is an ancient port, perfectly situated for the smuggler's trade, and the town is full of small pubs with dark corners and mysterious recesses.

As a matter of fact I've been reading the history of my new parish, and there's no doubt that a lot of smuggling has gone on in the past. French wines and brandy were the favourite articles of contraband for several centuries, but in the 17th and 18th centuries — the Penal Days — it seems that Catholic priests were smuggled into England, and the forebears of my present parishioners must have run serious risks by their continued law-breaking.

A delightful incident in the history of this town took place in 1855. Free tickets for a circus were given to all the coastguards of Shoreham-by-Sea. During the performance a huge consignment of contraband was landed unhindered in the town centre! There must have been raucous laughter in the pubs that night and the circus clowns would surely not have paid for a single drink.

I am glad that my new parishioners have smugglers among their ancestors. It will help them to understand that law-breaking is not always sinful, that Christians must sometimes be criminal in order to be authentic, that God's law of love is greater than any human legislation.

Perhaps it will also help them to understand how the debt crisis is the cause of so much suffering in Latin America, as well as in Africa and Asia. Your countries are beggaring and starving themselves to pay the interest on huge debts owed to a handful of wealthy nations. There is something very imoral about the whole situation, even though the debts are "legal" and refusal to pay is tantamount to breaking international laws. But then the crucifixion of Jesus Christ was also "legal".

Here at St. Peter's church we too have our debt. We owe the Midland Bank more than a third of a million pounds for a brand-new church and hall. Should we default and refuse to pay? I think not, because in our case the debt is just — we have received good value for the borrowed money.

In your case, however, the debt that is crippling your economies and impoverishing your people was unjustly incurred, without your knowledge and without giving you any tangible benefits. You must not pay. You must be law-breakers in order to be faithful to your consciences.

You must be smugglers on a massive scale if you are to remain alive, because the laws of the banks and the multinational companies in the 1980s are as outrageous as the laws that forbade the importation of French brandy and Catholic priests in the not-so-distant history of this country.

I pray that in your struggle you will be strengthened with God's grace, our solidarity — and a few circus clowns.

Affectionately,
John Medcalf

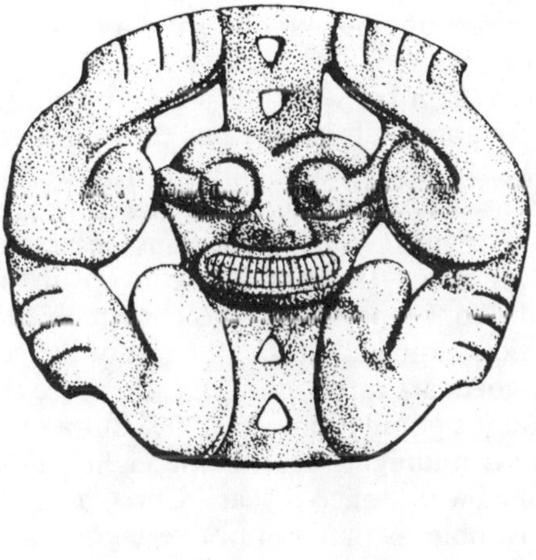

St. Peter's Church
Shoreham-By-Sea
West Sussex
Inglaterra
December, 1988

Dear Friends in Nicaragua,

For some strange reason I am dreading the Midnight Mass this Christmas. Last year it was horrific, but simple. The war made things simple and stark, and we prayed hard for real and lasting peacc in Nicaragua. Many of you prayed fervently and spontaneously for "a better President of the USA who will stop attacking our country".

I recall how the Sandinista soldiers came to Midnight Mass at Washtub Village and how you shared with them your meagre supplies of rice and beans in the meal that became a big celebration of life and love.

Remember how Doña Elvira was the back half of an ox in the nativity play performed during the mass? And how she came apart because her husband Don Carlos walked off in the opposite direction? Everybody roared with laughter and we forgot for a few hours the kidnappings, the torture, the killing. We were practising together what liberation theologians have called "the ministry of consolation", and a lot of people needed a lot of consoling.

Here at Shoreham-by-Sea things are much less simple. Everybody talks about Christmas but they all mean very different things when they use the same word. For most children, Christmas means school holidays and expensive presents from their parents. For most youths it means endless parties and entertainment. Parents feel obliged to keep up high buying standards and shopkeepers are wholeheartedly dedicated to selling on a scale unequalled during the rest of the year.

The church-goers are a tiny minority, no more than five per cent of Shoreham's population of 22,000. But we all know that at the Christmas midnight services the eight churches of the town will be filled with "once-a-year" Christians.

One of my troubles is that I'm not very good at formal sermons. I prefer to tell stories, and to let people guess the meaning and apply it to themselves. I think that the Catholics at St. Peter's are getting used to my odd way of preaching, but I suppose I'll have to be more formal and "more English" at the Midnight Mass, because of the "once-a-year" Christians.

And yet, perhaps I am being a coward. Maybe I ought to hire a real donkey and a full-grown ox and install them both on top of the expensive red carpet that covers our sanctuary. Instead of using incense perhaps I should let the natural animal smells fill the nostrils of everybody in the building that cost us a third of a million pounds. Finally I ought to invite the "winos" who sleep rough on the beach to burst in as "shepherds", to add even more realism to our Christmas worship.

I shall probably do none of these things — at least not this year. But Doña Elvira of Washtub village will know what I mean, and her great fall from grace with Don Carlos last year will for ever remind me that Jesus is the smile and the laughter on every care-worn face.

Feliz Navidad
John Medcalf

1989

St. Peter's Church
Shoreham-By-Sea
West Sussex
Inglaterra

6 January 1989

Dear Friends in Nicaragua,

Epiphany is a good time for writing to friends overseas. Transatlantic jets, like winged camels, will carry my words to you in Peru, Ecuador, Guatemala and Nicaragua, but I'm afraid there will be no gold, frankincense or myrrh.

Here in England the Three Kings have a low profile, as if people suspected their authenticity. The poetry of the story has been overlooked.

But I know how important Epiphany is to the people of Lima and other South American cities. Every *barrio* will select its "Gringo" King (any pale-faced boy will do), its "Sambo" King (boot-polish on his face if there aren't any real black boys available) and the "Cholo" King (90 per cent of Lima's children are "mestizo" or mixed-blood "cholos"). The Boy-Kings will cavort through the streets dressed in coloured ponchos, wearing paper crowns, and usually end up in the church at the beginning of the Epiphany Mass.

And we all know what it means. The world is one, but diverse. This planet of ours is multicoloured and beautiful — and God is colour-blind (except in South Africa).

A few weeks ago I visited a Catholic Secondary School in a town called Slough. I talked about the Third World, but a fifth-year boy from Jamaica objected to his country being called a Third World country.

On my way back to Shoreham-by-Sea I travelled in a third-class rail compartment (officially called "standard" by those whose job it is to paper over the cracks of this very class-conscious country), and I understood what the Jamaican boy was getting at. "Third World" means for him, and for many others, third class, third rate, standard.

The carriage was overcrowded and friendly for most of the journey, whereas the next carriage (first class) had scarcely half-a-dozen passengers, all of whom were sleeping or reading. I began to think that perhaps things weren't too bad, after all; we'd all get to our destination at about the same time. Perhaps the world was like that.

And then I was jolted from my reveries by a train roaring past in the opposite direction, and my image changed. We are not all on the same train, albeit in compartments of differing comfort. We are on different trains, going in opposite directions. The rich nations of the world are getting richer, and expect always to get richer, without let or hindrance. The poor countries of the Third World get poorer, and have no other expectations.

How far we are from the poetry of the Epiphany! The Three Kings are like the three Worlds, into which economists and politicians divide our planet. There is no time to look for three boys of different colours in Shoreham-by-Sea this year.

Perhaps I'll be content to put a large globe on the altar for the Mass of Epiphany, and I'll lift it up together with the host and the chalice and pray that there may one day be just One World.

Affectionately,

John Medcalf

Note: Several months later John Medcalf returned to Central America.

Abbey of the Crucified Saviour
Esquipulas
Guatemala
Central America

July 7, 1989

Dear Parishioners in Shoreham-by-Sea,

This is a land of forests, volcanoes, traditional Catholicism, enthusiastic sects and oven-fresh martyrs. Last Friday I tried to climb a safely-extinct volcano and lost my spectacles in the attempt. There are certain advantages in looking at Guatemala without spectacles, and I suspect that most of the American tourists who enjoy this "land of eternal spring" as the brochures describe it are as short-sighted as I was until a local optician restored my vision yesterday morning.

Last Friday (June 30) was also Army Day. Everybody has a "Day" in Latin America, from mothers-in-law to deep sea divers, and the celebrations usually include some kind of a "fiesta" and perhaps a special mass at the local church.

The prospect of witnessing celebrations for the Guatemalan Army—accused by the latest Amnesty International report of currently averaging 20 killings or "disappearances" a month—is what decided me to tackle an extinct volcano far from the madding crowd.

However, the loss of the spectacles turned everything topsy-turvy. I returned to the city of Antigua just in time to witness the conclusion of a massive religious demonstration in the largest church of the former capital city. There was not a colonel or a sergeant to be seen, at least not in uniform. The church was packed with "campesinos" or peasant farmers from the outlying villages beyond the volcanoes, and they had come to town to celebrate not Army Day, but Martyrs' Day. By one of those ironic and inexplicable quirks that so typify life here, Latin America Army Day and Martyrs' Day had coincided. You could pay your money and take your pick between the goose-stepping infantry battalions filling the central plaza and the hushed Maya Indians inside the church of San Francisco de Antigua.

I had missed the sermon, but mimeographed copies were being eagerly circulated round the vast basilica. Monsignor José Ramiro Pellecer, surrounded by ten priests of the deanery, spoke of the Emperors Nero and Diocletian, and of the catacombs in distant Rome. Martyrdom was not only a characteristic of the Early Church: it was its hallmark, its most potent proof to those whose faith was "for this life alone".

The hundreds of priests, nuns and catechists massacred by the Guatemalan Army in this present decade is another chapter of glory for the Universal Church, declared the prelate. The chief difference, he said, between the persecutors of the Roman Empire and those of present-day Guatemala, is that the first never thought of themselves as followers of Christ, whereas the latter have the effrontery to call themselves Christians.

Instead of the traditional bidding-prayers, each parish priest read out the list of those killed in his parish. After each name there was a silence, followed by a heartfelt chorus: "Señor, ten piedad de nosotros, Aleluya". "Lord have mercy on us; praised be the Lord".

I emerged into the sunlight, without spectacles but filled with hope. After all, the Roman Canon of the Mass (Number One in the present-day missal) is full of the names of those who fed the lions with their bodies in the Coliseum of Rome. The modern lions of Central America are no less real, and the witness—"usque ad sanguinem"—of so many humble Christians deserves the attention and the solidarity of the entire world.

My final days in Guatemala—before my departure to El Salvador tomorrow—are being spent in the relative tranquility of a large and beautiful Benedictine Abbey—that of Esquipulas. It was here that five Central American Presidents signed a solemn peace agreement in 1986 which might have succeeded had it not been torpedoed by the Reagan Administration in Washington.

I recall the beginning of Psalm 121:

"I lift up my eyes to the hills from whence comes my help."

The hills here are mostly volcanoes; some are extinct, but some are rumbling with a fire that could at any time erupt.

John Medcalf

McDonald's
Downtown San Salvador
El Salvador
Central America

July 28, 1989

Dear Friends in Shoreham-by-Sea,

This red plastic emporium of fast food is the safest place for writing letters in downtown San Salvador. Somehow one feels instinctively that the consumers of Big Macs and strawberry milkshakes will be spared the bullets and bombs of government or rebels in this Beirutish city of rapidly escalating violence. Instincts can be wrong.

Crossing the border by land from Guatemala last Thursday was surprisingly simple. Nobody else, apart from a few truck drivers, was coming into the country. The customs officials stamped my passport with a flourish and waved me into the only country in the world officially named after Jesus Christ the Saviour of the World, a country shunned by tourists for ten years because of a genocidal war that has turned nearly a quarter of its five million population into refugees.

San Salvador (''Holy Saviour'') is, like Beirut, two capital cities in one. They are divided not by religion but by social status. The wealthy live in the upper foothills of the saucer-shaped valley; the poor majority live in the depressed centre of the saucer where exhaust fumes and sewage pervade streets also filled with vendors and their wares.

An earthquake in 1986 has added an apocalyptic effect to the divided city: office-blocks and churches tilt at dangerous angles like towers of Pisa, the fallen plaster revealing twisted concrete columns and an occasional tiled toilet too public for use.

One afternoon I visited a wealthy family near the rim of the saucer. They had once been to Shoreham-by-Sea. All the talk was of ''the terrorist war,'' of how the new government (installed June 1) of Alfredo Cristiani would ''have to be firm with the rebels, and how everybody *(''todo el mundo'')* was converting to the evangelical sects ''because the Catholic Church is too mixed up in politics.'' They were dismayed that I had chosen to stay in a downtown hotel where I would ''have an ugly impression of San Salvador.''

On Saturday night the streets were deserted by 9 pm; an unofficial curfew is observed by the frightened population. The newspapers reported 15 assassinations for the previous day, including three children killed by a bomb. "Unknown criminals" is the nearest the journalist comes to an accusation.

Today is Sunday. I went to the cathedral at 8 am when Archbishop Rivera Damas (successor to the martyred Archbishop Oscar Romero) celebrated a 90-minute long Mass to at least a thousand downtowners. The atmosphere was unselfconsciously devout in spite of the insensitivity of the television cameramen. Two women in their thirties handed a large envelope to the prelate as he approached his throne; the cameras zoomed in to capture their faces, but the women were unconcerned. Petitions for investigation into "disappeared" husbands and sons are regularly handed to celebrants during Mass.

The archbishop's homily rambled exegetically through the gospel passage of the day—why the 72 disciples wore sandals, carried no wallets or Access cards, ate what was put in front of them, said "Shalom" only to the real lovers of peace.

The archbishop lamented the rise in the cost of basic foods, he named those whose assassinations had been investigated by church authorities, and he denounced the undoubted escalation of the Salvadorian conflict.

As I lined up to receive communion behind a woman who smelt of the fish she probably sold in the market, I felt proud to belong to this church of the poor. The sects, so well financed by American tele-evangelists, will probably win over an increasing proportion of those who live materially well on the rim of the saucer.

Catholicism will be left with those dismissed as the slops and the dregs—the street vendors, the homeless, the peasant farmers, the displaced refugees with nothing to lose in this life but their pain and sorrow.

The Catholic Church in El Salvador is creating a faithful remnant of men and women who are following the steps of the Saviour after whom their country is named.

John Medcalf

A Windowless Cell
Honduras
Central America
August 4, 1989

Dear Friends at Shoreham-by-Sea,

If I had thought to use my Peruvian passport I would not be in a Honduran jail tonight. It all began at midday when I tried to cross by land from El Salvador into a country that means literally "The Depths"—or better perhaps "The Pits". To travel by land to Nicaragua it is necessary to pass through a strip of Honduras 100 miles long.

I showed the Honduran frontier guard my British passport. I won't say he snorted, but the sound he uttered when he saw my Nicaraguan residency permit was certainly on the borderline of a snort.

- Your passport is full of communist visas, he said.
- There's only one, and that's hardly communist, I replied cautiously.
- Well you can't stay in Honduras.
- I didn't really want to.
- Well we can't take the risk. You'll have to be escorted to the Nicaraguan frontier and the police officer who goes with you will keep your passport. That's the law.

I felt like telling him it was a very peculiar law. Was there an officially declared war between Honduras and Nicaragua? What about the Esquipulas Peace Agreement permitting free passage between the five republics of Central America? Was I a contagious microbe?

The questions remained on the inner side of my lips; I didn't want any more of his near snorts, or worse. At least I was not to be turned back to El Salvador, and at least I was going to travel in the right direction—towards Nicaragua Libre.

One hour and 20 dollars later I was on a bus with the police escort sitting behind me. The 20 dollars were supposed to be for "travelling expenses" but there was no receipt forthcoming. Next to me sat a young British photographer whose virgin passport had incurred no snorts or sanctions at the Honduran frontier.

We travelled across The Depths in the worst hours of the heat, and it took us a total of four vehicles to reach the Nicaraguan border. I spoke en route with a schoolteacher, a national serviceman and several policemen. They all had this in common: a strong desire to get out of Honduras at the earliest opportunity and start a new life in the USA.

Land frontiers are a bit like post offices or supermarkets; they tend to close at about 6 pm. Unfortunately for us it was close to 7 pm and we were in a miserable little border town called San Marcos. We are still there now, a few hours later. The police guard, whose name we have discovered is Henry, has taken us to this seedy one-storey building with a shop frontage and a series of small windowless rooms behind. The photographer and I have a bed apiece and a naked light bulb of the lowest wattage. Henry is next door (dreaming of sky-scrapers in New York perhaps) and I just hope and pray that tomorrow I shall receive back my British passport and will be able to cross the border to Nicaragua.

I have also found a new meaning to Psalm 130:

"Out of The Depths I cry to thee O Lord,
Lord, hear my voice..."

Affectionately,
John Medcalf

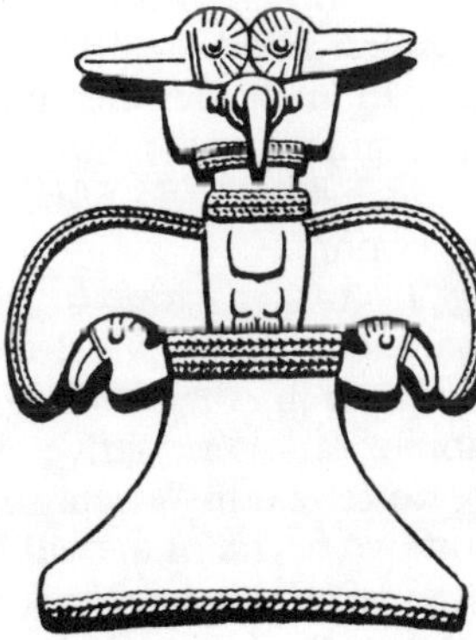

Los Antojitos Restaurant
Managua
Nicaragua
Central America

August 11, 1989

Dear Friends,

My last letter, from a windowless cell in Honduras, may have caused concern. In fact my police escort, Henry, behaved quite well the following morning, finding us a hearty breakfast of beans and rice (which I had to pay for of course) before escorting the photographer and myself to the Nicaraguan frontier a short distance along a pot-holed road. As I crossed over I felt like a goldfish slithering from a cat's paw back into the pond.

Everything in Nicaragua betokened the approaching Tenth Anniversary of the Sandinista Revolution. Instead of the huge Coca-Cola billboards common to other countries of the region we saw the official anniversary poster showing a black and red heart with the words "never was there so much patriotism in one heart".

In Managua I met Hugh O'Shaughnessy, the Latin American correspondent for *The Observer,* and we drove east to Rama in his hired Toyota, calling in to see an impressively happy orphanage at Juigalpa with 78 children of all ages (many orphaned by the present war) whose clothes and toys were being provided by the Catholics of Grimsby in England.

In Rama we had first-hand evidence of the devastation caused by Hurricane Joan in October last year. A dynamic mayor, Samuel Mejía, and a local team with technical aid from Holland and Austria, are helping to re-house the 10,000 or so inhabitants of this river port.

The following day I returned alone to Muelle de los Bueyes (Ox-ford) where I had been parish priest for nearly three years until my return to England in April 1988. Fr. Bernard Boulang was visiting his mother in their native Normandy and the American nuns were on retreat in Wisconsin, all of which helps to explain why within two hours of arrival I found myself staring down at six corpses lying side by side for identification purposes on the concrete floor of the village hall. I was back on duty.

The story was bizarre. It seems that a platoon of "contras" had stumbled upon an isolated farmstead where there was music and dancing. A girl was celebrating her 15th birthday, and a pig had been killed and roasted in her honour. The "contra" soldiers took over the house and the fiesta, but not before they had been observed by a patrol of Sandinista militia. What followed is far from clear, but there was a skirmish in which four uniformed "contras" were killed as well as two civilians, including the 15 year old girl. The bodies were brought in to Ox-ford the following morning.

I had the only camera in the village, so I photographed the dead "contras" as well as the civilians. Putrefaction had already set in and it was obvious that continued exposure of the corpses in a humid heat of well over 30°C was a health hazard for the population. On the other hand a fair time had to be given for possible identification by relatives or friends.

In the end the six persons were buried that evening. The carpenters of the town (unfortunately well accustomed to this routine over the past decade) had hurriedly made individual coffins of unplaned planks of wood. A large crowd had gathered. I read aloud the story from John II of the resurrection of Lazarus (the reference to the stench of the corpse was particularly apt).

I said the prayers for the dead and for peace in Central America. The bodies were taken away to the cemetery accompanied by the grieving relatives of the girl who was killed on the very day that by Latin American tradition should have been the happiest day of her life.

This sad home-coming to a village I had grown to love was a reminder to me that things have not changed very much here since I left. It is clear that the "contras" are being kept in fighting form by the USA until the elections on February 25 next year. Should the Nicaraguans dare to vote for another term of "Sandinismo" then the "contras" would still be there to keep the war going and to tie up half the Nicaraguan budget in the costly defence of a democratically elected government.

A few days later I was present at a happier occasion in the vast Carlos Fonseca plaza of Managua. It was July 19, exactly ten years since the Sandinistas took over from the corrupt 45-year dictatorship of the Somoza family. The event reminded me in some respects of the Billy Graham mission I had attended a few weeks before at Crystal Palace in London. There was the same sense of expectation, the rousing music, the cheering, the euphoria.

President Daniel Ortega is not as skilled an orator as Dr. Graham or Fidel Castro, but the 300,000 flag-waving people seemed to inspire and strengthen him with their enthusiasm. One of his phrases in the 50-minute speech was: "where the people are, there too is God".

And this, to my mind, says it all. Humanly speaking there seems little or no reason for hope in the battered republics of Central America. Three centuries of Spanish colonialism have been followed by a century and a half of bullying from the USA. The struggle for independence and dignity is ridiculously unequal, and the cost in human lives incalculable. But these people have an inner strength that is contagious. Their religion is no alienating opium. Their God is not in the clouds, nor in a Swiss bank account. He is written large and bold in the faces of the poor.

Affectionately
John Medcalf

MISA CAMPESINA

(Peasant Farmers' Mass)
Spanish Text & Music
by Carlos Mejía Godoy

ENTRANCE SONG

You are the God of the poor
the God who is human and simple
the God who perspires in the market
the God with a face that is wrinkled.
So I can talk to you plainly
and speak in the words of my people
for you are the God-become-Worker
for you are the Carpenter-Christ.

You walk hand in hand with my people
you sweat in the fields and in the city
you join in the line of workers at sundown
to receive the day's wage for your labour.
You munch sweetened ice on the street-corner
with Eusebio, Pancho and Juan José
and you even add your voice to their protests
when the ice is sour instead of sweet.

I have seen you in the shop on the corner
I have seen you sweeping the street before dawn
selling newspapers outside the stadium,
never for a moment ashamed that you're poor.
I have seen you as a gas station attendant
checking the tires of a fine limousine
I have seen you in a gang of road workers
or in a factory oiling a machine.

KYRIE

Jesus, Jesus, Our Lord,
be on our side and support us
Jesus, Jesus, Our Lord,
be on our side and support us.
Jesus, Jesus, Our Lord
show solidarity
not with the class that oppresses
that kills and represses
the people you love,
but with the class that is cheated
enslaved and ill-treated
and longs for your peace.

GLORIA

With the most explosive music of my country we sing and shout
Glory to Christ Jesus, who loves a fiesta without a doubt.
Let all of us sing to the Lord who is leader of truth and light
with exuberance and madness, just as fireworks banish sadness
lighting up the sky with gladness
in the fiesta of the poor.

Glory to God in Honduras, Costa Rica, Guatemala,
El Salvador, Panama and Nicaragua.
Glory to God in Belize, Mexico and Cuba
and all the many islands of the Caribbean Sea.

Glory to him who follows the light of Christ's own Gospel,
who is fearless in fighting grave injustice.
Glory to him who suffers in prison or in exile
and lays his life down for the hungry and the weak.

Lord we give you glory with the sound of the marimbas
with the large one-stringed quijongos
with guitars and big brass drum
from the Pacific and Atlantic coastlands
with all the songs and dances of our Nicaraguan home.

CREDO

I do believe most sincerely
that God our Parent has really
engendered everything,
that his artistic creation
and his love-filled contemplation
are the reason why we sing:
songs to the stars and the moonlight
ballads to lovers at midnight
sailing-boats on rivers as they
float down quietly to the sea;
coffee and cotton plantations,
food and drink for all occasions
and the mutilated forests
where there's no ecology.

I BELIEVE
IN A GOD WHO IS A CRAFTSMAN
BUILDER, CARPENTER AND DRAFTSMAN,
ARCHITECT AND ENGINEER.
I BELIEVE
IN A GOD WHOSE WHOLE CREATION
IS A CONSTANT REVELATION
OF HIS JUSTICE AND HIS LOVE.

I do believe that Christ Jesus,
light of God's light, came to free us
from all that makes us slaves.
True Son of God and our Brother
born of pure Mary our Mother
by his redemption we're saved.
By his own village rejected
dismissed as a fool, clown and devil
laughed at by priests and lawyers
followed by sinners and the poor,
sold by a friend-become-traitor
denied by the fisherman Peter
accused by ambitious churchmen
condemned by a puppet from Rome.

I do believe in a Saviour
human in all his behaviour
worker, companion and friend.
His death and his resurrection
offer us true liberation
bringing to birth the New Man.
He is alive, he is risen
in every arm that is lifted
to defend the poor and helpless
from the exploiter's mighty power.
He is alive in the farmstead
in the shanty-town by the river,
I do believe that he'll never
abandon the friends that he loves!

SONG OF MEDITATION

Before the day has broken
the birds begin their chorus,
they are awake before us
to sing their Maker's praises.
The tapping on a tree-trunk
is just the green woodpecker
as he carves a simple dwelling
way beyond the reach of menacing foes,
while a crimson-coated humming-bird
prepares to plunge into a wild rose.

I too would add my music
to praise my true Companion
and echo through the canyon
his song of peace and love.
A thousand times I thank him
for being so rebellious
and fighting night and day
against injustice, without hatred in his heart.

Central Americans
united in our chorus
arriving from our farmsteads
with our knapsacks and our purses full of love.
You are our sun and moon
to guide us through the forest,
with you we cannot fail, for you go on before us.

Sing through the tropics
all you parrots and canaries
the multicoloured parakeets, white herons
and the crimson-topped macaw.
Hear the sparrow-hawk
the hungry turkey-buzzard
raise their voices to heaven
and God is pleased to hear them.

CREDO

Workers from the town and country
with the bread and wine
we offer what we've sown:
almonds, oranges and lemons
coconuts and melons
which our land has grown;
breadfruit, grapefruit, passion-
fruit and luscious mangos
coloured like the sun,
tamarinds and ripe bananas
which the hands of farmers
gather safely home.

All that I have to give
I give you freely:
all my waiting, all my walking
all my love of talking
all my will to live.
All that I have to give
I give you freely
all my energy and laughter
hopes of life hereafter
all my love, O Lord.

Working people from all nations
who have toiled in patience
since the world began,
farmers, foresters and ploughmen
fishermen and seamen,
woman, child and man;
all those unemployed who long for
work and know it's wrong for
governments to plan
massive unemployment for the poor
who look no further than their daily bread.

SANCTUS

On every path and highway
wherever people gather
I see the face of Jesus
the image of your truth;
for you are three times holy
for you are three times righteous,
take off the yoke of bondage
give us our liberty.

You walk beside your people,
the clouds are not your dwelling;
you practise love and justice
Good Shepherd of your sheep;
for you are three times holy
for you are three times righteous,
take off the yoke of bondage,
give us our liberty.

COMMUNION SONG

Let's go to the harvest
to the harvest of the Lord,
Jesus Christ invites us
to his harvest feast of love;
maizefields all around us
glisten in the sun —
Let's go to the harvest
to the harvest of the Lord!

People encircle the altar
hungry for God's living food,
knowing that sharing this banquet
will make us companions of body and blood.
I've come from near the volcano
next to the palm-tree lagoon,
farm-workers' dances and prances
with typical rhythm and tropical tune.

All the wild life of the lakeside
joins in our giving of thanks,
even the fish leap for joy and fraternity
swimming right up to the banks.
Tasty bass, large alligators,
wild duck and low-flying gulls
even the smallest sardines seem to dance
as they dream at the feast of the fools.

Holy Communion is never
any ordinary thing,
rather it means dedication
to bring to each people and nation
God's love;
so that you share in the struggle
of all humanity
Stand up and say: I'm a Christian
and that means that you can depend on me!

SONG OF FAREWELL

There is nothing more inspiring than to see
the people all united
resolving all their problems and their pains
with no one uninvited;
there is nothing more inspiring than to hear
the song of heartfelt pleasure
from a great fraternal shout
that nobody can measure.

There is not a prettier sight in all the world
than a hundred farmers
with their wives and with their parents and (best of all!)
with their little charmers;
from where I am sitting I can see — guess who!
Farmer Gonzalez!
With all his chubby children
singing songs of praise!

It is hard to say Adios
at the finish of a fiesta
there's a lump right in my throat
that will vanish with a siesta;
but this sadness soon will pass
and change to joy and laughter
when we all meet up again
at the banquet of our Master!

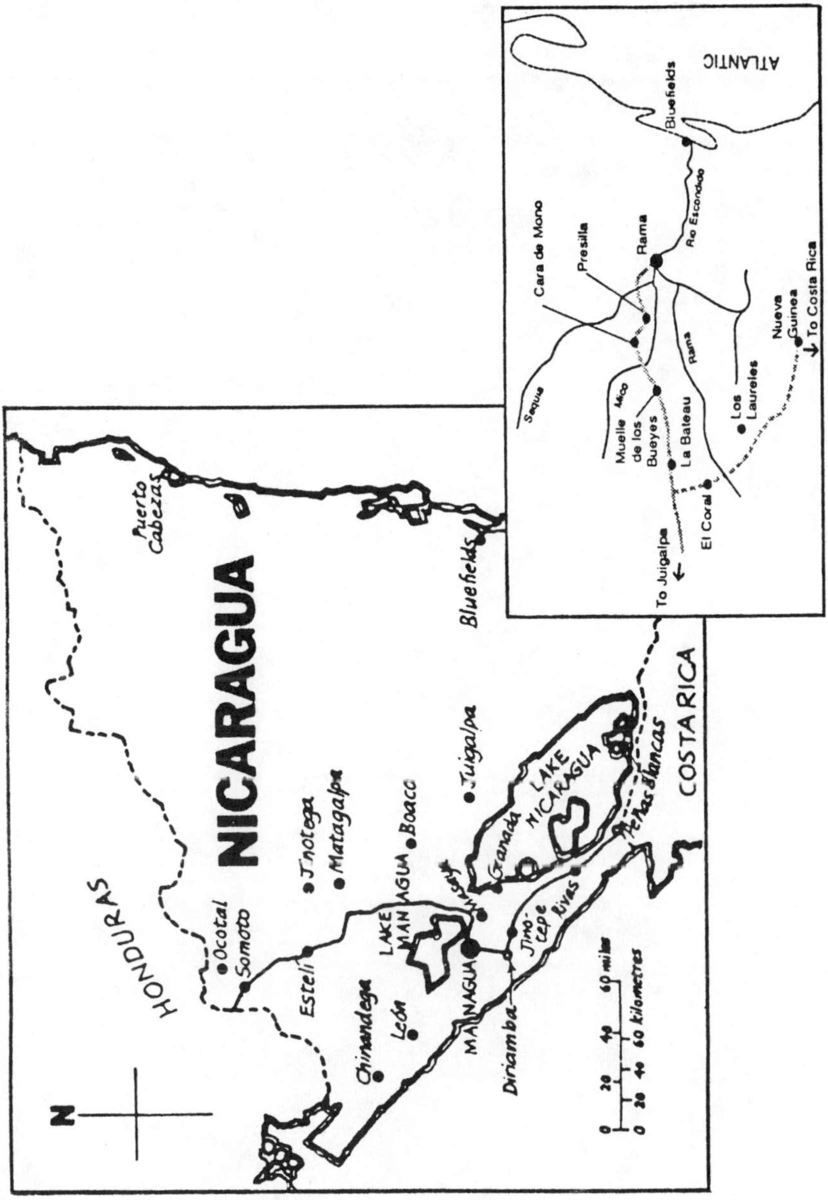
NICARAGUA
HONDURAS
COSTA RICA
N
Ocotal
Somoto
Estelí
Chinandega
León
Jinotega
Matagalpa
Boaco
Juigalpa
LAKE MANAGUA
MANAGUA
Masaya
Granada
Diriamba
Jinotepe
Rivas
LAKE NICARAGUA
Peñas Blancas
Bluefields
Puerto Cabezas
0 20 40 60 miles
0 20 40 60 kilometres
ATLANTIC
Cara de Mono
Presilla
Rama
Rio Escondido
Seguia
Mico
Rama
Muelle de los Bueyes
La Bateau
El Coral
Los Laureles
Nueva Guinea
To Juigalpa
To Costa Rica